Human Training

A User Guide to You

A handy manual for business adulting, living in the world of people, and generally being a decent human

ISBN: 979-8-9853145-0-2

DEDICATION

For all of those amazing people who taught me along the way; those who laughed with me, those who laughed at me, and especially those who took some of the same steps.

Table of Contents

Acknowledgments 5

Introduction 7

PART I: Work Is Work 11

Chapter 1: Put Your Phone Down 13

Chapter 2: Read the Damn Email 16

Chapter 3: Ghoster 19

Chapter 4: Bad Mouthing 23

Chapter 5: Do Your Damn Job 27

Chapter 6: What Are You Worth? 32

Chapter 7: Communication 37

Chapter 8: Meetings 44

Chapter 9: Managing 49

Chapter 10: Leading 55

Chapter 11: Do What You Say 60

Chapter 12: Workplace Love 64

Chapter 13: Mentors 67

Chapter 14: The Magic of Teams 71

Chapter 15: Taking the Back Seat 74

Chapter 16: Own It 76

PART II: It's All About You 79

Chapter 17: Be You, Just Less 81

Chapter 18: Habit Forming 84

Chapter 19: Hard Things & Scary Things 86

Chapter 20: Time 91

Chapter 21: How Do You Recharge? 95

Chapter 22: Career Choices 98

Chapter 23: Undisciplined Thing 101

Chapter 24: You Made Your Point 105

Chapter 25: Know When to Hush 109

Chapter 26: Read the Room 113

Chapter 27: Don't Fix Everything 117

Chapter 28: Shut Up (and Listen) 120

Chapter 29: The Millennial Excuse 122

Chapter 30: You Got Screwed 125

Chapter 31: Who ARE You? 127

PART III: Just No 133

Chapter 32: Don't Be an Ass 135

Chapter 33: Are You a Dark Cloud? 139

Chapter 34: Don't BS 143

Chapter 35: Social Media 145

Chapter 36: Don't Be Stupid 149

Chapter 37: You're Wearing That? 151

Chapter 38: Strength & Power 156

Chapter 39: Words Matter 160

Chapter 40: Dude Bros & Empty Girls 164

Chapter 41: Mansplaining 166

Chapter 42: Don't Be Gross 171

Chapter 43: When No One Is Looking 174

PART IV: It's Not About You 177

Chapter 44: Judging the Book 179

Chapter 45: My Group Is Better 183

Chapter 46: Perspective 185

Chapter 47: White People 189

Chapter 48: Black People 193

Chapter 49: Other People 198

Chapter 50: The Gender Spectrum 202

Chapter 51: The Only Sexuality… 205

Chapter 52: About Men 207

Chapter 53: About Women 213

Chapter 54: Out Front 224

Chapter 55: Free Speech Isn't Free 226

Chapter 56: Religion 228

PART V: Leveling Up 231

Chapter 57: Evolve 233

Chapter 58: No, YOU'RE Biased! 237

Chapter 59: Nonbinary World 240

Chapter 60: That Sounds Right 242

Chapter 61: The Power of Numbers 244

Chapter 62: Go Look It Up 250

Chapter 63: Signal in the Noise 252

Chapter 64: Argue the Other Side 255

Chapter 65: It's a Measure, Not a Target 257

Chapter 66: The Pool 259

Chapter 67: Attack the Message 261

Chapter 68: Zero-Sum Game 264

Chapter 69: A World of Difference 266

Chapter 70: Giving Back 269

The Wrap 273

About the Author 275

Acknowledgments

The list of people who helped me become who I am today is long, and I will fail to include everyone who matters. Acknowledging that failure in advance lets me move on and actually write this acknowledgement.

My parents, a Marine officer who served in Vietnam and a hippy who protested that same war, live vividly in my head, guiding and explaining so much about me. My amazing, long-suffering wife (suffering me) and my brilliant daughters are the reason that I am any sort of decent human at this point.

My brother and sisters, and those 10 other people who put up with me enough to be inside the inner circle of the hell that accompanies knowing me. And of course, the people who read this book in advance, challenging, questioning, improving. I did none of this without all of you, and I thank you all.

Introduction

There are people who read the manual and people who don't, and some in between who will read it only if they get stuck. This manual is for all of you.

I wrote "Human Training," in some sense, to me, to the me who started fresh out of graduate school and somehow screwed up everything, at least a little, on the way to now. If I had this book in my hands early in my journey, so many things would have been better, easier, smoother, and made more sense. Since I can't travel in time, I hope to help you now.

I am not trying to change you, or trying to get you to be like me, or to be someone else. This is central to everything that follows, and I can't emphasize it enough.

My one and only goal is to give you a "User Guide to You." A tool that guides the right way for you, not the right way for someone else. A tool to help make it easier to be you; to be the best you that you can be. A tool to share some insight, some tips, some hindsight, some benefits of trials by fire, and even some trial and error. When you get to the end of the book, I hope *your* journey becomes a bit easier, happier, and more successful.

Awareness is so important to all of this – awareness of yourself and the world around you. The key to success is based on your ability to look in the mirror and really see you, not someone else, and not an idealized version of yourself.

This awareness is the biggest hurdle to self-improvement, and once you get past that, you have to get over the next big hurdle: caring enough about fixing it to make it a priority.

If you get one useful idea; if you find one chapter that makes your life better or easier, then I have succeeded. And for those of you who will shake your heads and say "Well, of course," to many of these chapters, this is great, you are already ahead.

And if things in this book irritate or offend you, if things I wrote make you angry or you don't believe them, it is possible I am wrong or that I phrased something poorly. I know this and apologize in advance. But it is also possible that what I said hits too close to home, is too close for comfort. Do you know that, and will you commit to that proverbial look in the mirror?

One huge caveat, since I am a completely out-of-the-closet data nerd: It's important to remember the idea of the "bell curve" throughout this book. When I say something about men, about women, about bosses, about anything, I am almost always talking about most of them, not all of them. The bell curve says a small number of people are one way, lots of people are in the middle, and a small number are the other way. So some drop out of high school, most people finish it, and some graduate from college. Some people are short, most are average, and some are giants. You get the idea. And you will see why I need to point this out; why I ask you to resist getting your panties in a bunch and writing some righteously indignant email to me. We're generalizing here, people.

There is so much fantastic research and writing about nearly everything in this book. Anything that makes you want more or that you have questions about, please, do go look. So many smart people have worked so hard to help us understand the world better and navigate it better.

This book is based on many years of my own research, reading, and direct experience in leading, managing, being led and managed, working solo, working in teams, in small organizations and large, in the corporate world, in government, in nonprofits, and in startups.

I resisted the temptation to get too deep into any of these topics, but the depth and nuance is out there. I wanted these chapters to be quick so I could cover a lot of ground in one book.

The chapters are short, to the point, and fast. They are intended for you to get in, get the idea, get out, and get on with your life. It means a great deal to me that you are here reading this. I wrote it for you. Let's get started.[1]

[1] Two notes I want to address: The first is about pronouns. I used traditional pronouns, as well as the modern usage of "they," interchangeably throughout this book. It was an intentional choice to flip back and forth between genders to avoid defaulting to one or the other, particularly given the range of topics where internal biases might send your fingers typing one way. And I wanted to integrate the singular usage of "they" to accommodate society's evolving approach to gender identity. And second, in recent years, most publications have begun capitalizing the use of "Black" when writing about race. Many of those same publications chose to keep "white" lower case. The rationale for both (mostly) makes sense to me, but every time I used white and Black in the same chapters, it just looked odd, so I made the editing choice to keep them both capitalized. There is no underlying meaning in my choice to capitalize "White" other than typographical consistency.

PART I: Work Is Work

If you're getting out of college soon and headed into the professional world, what do you already know about that world? Where did you pick up this information? Maybe you had an internship, so you got a first-hand taste of what's to come. Maybe all your information came from reading and movies, from friends, or your parents.

If you are in the workforce already, but still new to it, where are you getting guidance? From co-workers, media, or bosses? Have you had some hard lessons already?

If you are experienced in the work world, but new to management or a new type of organization, what guides you? It's still new territory for you, after all.

These chapters are designed to help you hit the ground running. I hope they are useful, and with some luck, let you stumble a whole lot less.

And maybe keep being a Decent Human Being along the way.

Chapter 1: Put Your Phone Down

She walked right into a wall and farted on impact. This is not something you share. You just tuck that one away in the Nobody Needs to Know That file and move on. But her young son saw it, and of course, thought it was the funniest thing in the history of the universe. It will be a story passed down in her family forever. But for us, it's about the cost of not paying attention.

Put your phone down: This one sounds easy, right? Obvious?

It's not. Our phones have become so integrated into the fabric of our lives that they are much like watches were for the past 100 years.

But that gets us exactly at the point here: Don't look at your watch. Have you ever been in a meeting or on a date, and caught someone glancing at their watch? Sucks. Even if it was for a good reason, it always looks and feels like that person is done with you, and has somewhere better to be, something better to do.

And now that most of us use the phone that way – to look at the time or to check in with the world – it carries the same cost.

There are two big reasons to be mindful of this one. The first, well, it's part of being a Decent Human Being. If you're talking to someone, talk to them. Listen to them. Pay attention to them. On top of being the decent human thing to do, it will also make you a wonderful magical person who *listens*. Unicorn-rare.

Imagine you're talking to someone, and then right in the middle of a sentence, they just turn and start talking to someone else, or answer the phone and start talking. Not cool. Looking at your phone is the same thing.

Now picture this: You sit down to talk with someone, at work, at home, on a date, wherever, and you place your phone down on the table, face down. Or you put it in your purse/pocket. It's a signal. A powerful one. I am paying attention to *you* right now. You are what matters.

For the exception-weasels out there wondering about their smart watches: Yes, it's the same. No looking.

And if there's something going on in your day that might *really* require an interruption – maybe you're waiting for an important call or text that you can't miss – state it upfront, and apologize in advance. "Hey, I'm waiting for the boss to call about a project and I can't miss it, so I'm sorry in advance if they call during our time because I'll need to grab it, but it'll be quick."

The second big reason to put down your phone is tactical. If you don't really care about my DHB (Decent Human Being) argument, and I truly hope that you do, at least by the end of this book, then do it to show people you are paying attention to them.

It's not just showing that you are paying attention to one person; this carries over to meetings, dinners, and really anything with other humans. It shows respect to family, to teachers, to bosses, to loved ones, to friends. Either realize this is an important way to show it, or at least understand that other people feel this way and do it anyway, even if you don't buy into why.

And to those of you, and there are many, who say they can multitask. I swear I can hear you saying it: That you are paying attention to the person in front of you *and* looking at a cat video. I say that's a giant turd of nonsense. Multitasking came, had its moment in the sun, and then faded as the research mounted that we just don't do that. We are really task-switching rapidly. And not efficiently.

One more idea: A sibling to putting your phone down is not looking at it at all. We all have gotten so used to it keeping us company at every waking moment, hell, maybe sleeping moments now too, that it's worth testing life here and there without it. Start small and don't freak out.

Next time you sit somewhere to just take a breath, leave your phone in your pocket and just be. Look around. Watch for the entertaining oddballs. Just for a few minutes. See how it goes. And when you're ready, try it in a coffee shop or somewhere like that. For the *whole* time you're there. This will help reduce your phone's role as a security blanket; as an excuse to avoid the world; as a reason to not look at anything. You will learn something about the world, and something about you.

Now what? You made it through Chapter 1. Easy, right? Keep going. These are all going to be fast. They are built for modern attention spans and for all those who think that a typical magazine article is TL;DR (too long; didn't read).

And since so many of you jumped right to Chapter 1 and skipped the Introduction: Let me make an impassioned plea right here that you go read it now. And if you just can't, here's the super-short version: This book is about helping you be *you*, just better, more efficient, more hassle-free. My goal is not to change who you are, but to give you some insight and tools to be a top-level DHB, and to experience all the happy things that will come from that, both internally and externally, in your life.

So read on. And thank you.

Chapter 2: Read the Damn Email

I know, I know, you get a ton of email every day. It never stops. Even when (if?) you get your inbox to zero, you get busy for a few hours and it refills, like water in a hole you dig at the beach. There are plenty of strategies to help manage this, and to get you started, this chapter will hit on a few. But that's not what it's really about.

It's about functioning in the world. It's about managing your work and your personal life in a way that works for you, not just for a moment, but for the long road. It's about showing respect and care for others.

Read the email. Seriously. Read the damn email. It's become so fundamental to our lives. Ignoring emails, skipping them, missing them, these things will cost you. It will cost you at work; it will cost you in life.

There are two parts to this: First, managing them; staying on top of the pile. That we'll come back to. The part we'll start with: *actually* reading them.

This is all on you. Everything else is an excuse. There are too many, you are too busy, most of them are not important. These are all true, but they are still excuses. And they ignore two parts of the reality: Lots of us are sort of lazy, and lots of us don't really care about anything outside of the narrow list of things we care about. If you care about being a Decent Human Being, then reading an email from someone you know is sort of required. So is responding to it. And if you want to be successful in your career, paying attention to what's in these emails, and responding to them, will help you far more than it costs in effort. You'll be regarded as more effective in your work, and you'll know what's going on. Two things that truly matter.

When I coach about this, I joke – really only half-joking – that a third of the people will read only the subject line, a third also will read the first paragraph, and most of the rest will not even see the email. And yes, there are a dedicated few who read every last word. You weirdos know who you are. We depend on you to point out the thing we didn't bother to read and will screw us over if we don't know it.

I encourage people to write a subject line that gets enough info across to get by. Important meeting tomorrow at 9 a.m., be there. Then in a tight summary, tell people what the meeting will accomplish and why they need to be there. Then you can say *all* the rest for those who want the detail and who like to be prepared. And if you add an attachment, good luck with that. Lots of people won't look at it. If the attachment is critical, then say that in the first paragraph and why. And if you can, summarize what's in the attachment there too.

If all this sounds like I coach people to work around a problem, I do.

There are lots of little things you can do to make it easier for others to manage their email load. Be careful about emails to large groups. Those replies and chains can become unwieldy and make everyone's eyes glaze over. This increases the risk that important things will be missed. When this happens, take it to a new email sent to smaller groups to manage a particular point. And don't keep using chains to add new topics. People will miss those because they are *so* done with the original subject. Start a new one. Don't be lazy.

Be clear, be brief, be accurate. If you battle your inbox, it might help to think about what *you* would appreciate in an email.

And to manage the torrent? Search the web for strategies, and you'll see a bunch. But start with this: Find a strategy that works for *you*. And then do it. Mine is this: I look at email and act on them. Then I leave them if I might need them later for reference, or delete them if I don't. And anything I haven't read yet, or I have but haven't acted on yet, I leave as unread. That always keeps me with a focused list of those that need my attention. I flag emails with time-bound things like tickets to events, flight schedules, or anything I will likely need and don't want to have to hunt for in the moment.

The other thing I do is use multiple email addresses: one for all those things in the world that want it, whether it's signing up, ordering, buying, whatever. Another email address I use only for work. Clutter aside, there are very good reasons not to use your work email for personal stuff. Ask IT and HR people how private that is. They might giggle. And a third one I use for personal stuff; for friends and family. This goes a long way toward keeping your inboxes manageable and less of a hassle. Plus you are far less likely to miss something that will bite you in the butt. And for the things-in-the-world email address, always remember to check/uncheck that pesky "bury me in junk email please" box when you sign up for something. If you still have too many, look into tools that will manage junk and even send you summaries. And here's where I'll make a plea for you to look in your spam folder every week. It will save you one day.

There are plenty of non-email tools now, mostly in two flavors: messaging platforms such as traditional text, WhatsApp, Facebook Messenger and so on. And we have collaboration platforms such as Slack and Teams. An easy rule of thumb is to use the messaging platforms for your personal life and the collaboration platforms for work and group activities. And keep those to brief exchanges. Save the long stuff for emails and actual live conversations (that's still a thing, really).

Back to the point: If you are not reading your email, you are not doing your job and/or being a DHB to friends and family. You are telling bosses, colleagues, friends, and family that whatever they are trying to tell you is just not that important to you.

If you don't want to be that person, find a way that works for you to stay on top of it. It'll be worth it.

Chapter 3: Ghoster

When you play peek-a-boo with a baby, and they are just beside themselves with delight every time you do it, science says there's a good reason for this: Babies haven't developed "object permanence" yet. They can't hold onto things in their little heads and live only in the moment. So when you cover your face with your hands, to them you are *gone*. And then you are back. It's magic, over and over.

Over the years, I've come to think about relationships that way. The closer somebody is to your everyday life, the more you think about them, the more you connect with them. But the more distant they get, for most of us, the more the connection fades.

So when your best friend in the whole world, someone you might see every day or talk to every day, moves away, you swear nothing will change. Maybe you keep it up for a while, but it drops off. It just does. What happened? Out of sight, out of mind – just like the babies.

You're not a bad person, but you have a certain amount of time, a certain amount of energy, and you will spend it on what's in front of you, what's important right now in your life. You still love that friend, and think the world of her, but she's gone, and everything else in your life is still there, demanding your attention. We prioritize our focus.

Ghosting: you've done it or it's happened to you, or both. You *know* what it is. But for the benefit of my mother, who wrote off the world and moved to a very rural spot in Central America: Ghosting is when someone reaches out and you ignore it. Voice, email, text, messaging – the platform doesn't matter. You just disappear, turn into a ghost.

For this chapter, let's look at two big ghosters: The selfish-focus type, and the notorious "deal with it by not dealing with it" type.

Ghosting is a shortcut. An easy way out that's driven by selfishness. We focus on ourselves. This focus is healthy in a lot of ways; after all, we do have to take care of us.

The word "selfish" has a bad smell to it, and rightly so most of the time. It can mean acting in your best interest at the expense of others. But it isn't black and white. It's a spectrum, like so many things in life (see Chapter 59, Nonbinary World). People who always do for others at their own expense pay a big price for that. And people who always do for themselves at the expense of others, well, no one likes them. There's a balance somewhere in there. And emotionally aware people give a little more when others really need it, and take a little more when they need it. It should ebb and flow depending on what life is throwing at you.

That "out of sight, out of mind" concept in our personal lives looks a little different at work. We are busy, so busy. We focus on what's right in front of us, the thing that's on fire. All the things that aren't on fire can take a backseat and get a little neglected.

You might be thinking that you don't have any choice, that you have to focus that way. And it's true, you probably do. But let me give you two things to think about here: First, *you* know why you're doing it, but all the people you are ignoring do not. To them, in your personal life and in this context at work, you come off like a jerk, like someone who doesn't care. Second is the practical impact of ignoring others. Aside from the hurt feelings you cause, you screw over other people's deadlines, their plans, their ability to get their work done. This matters to them, and it affects the team, and the organization.

A slightly different struggle: The Deep Focus. I have a friend who gets lost in her work. She'll go for hours buried in something and ghost all sorts of people without even thinking about it. I used to get mildly irritated at this, but then found out she would also forget to go to the bathroom or eat or get coffee, and realized it was not about me at all.

Yet another type: The Forgetter. Like The Deep Focus, there's no malicious intent here; it's not meant as disrespect or selfishness. But it can sure look like it; feel like it. There are lots of us who just forget things. It's just the way we are. But regardless of the reason, you end up ghosting people and it sucks.

No matter why and how you ghost, it will hurt you too, not just other people. It will cost you with friends, with family, in relationships, and in your career. Maybe not every time, but it will cost you.

What can you do? What should you do? The first step is simple, maybe not easy, but simple. Just keep reminding yourself that your actions are impacting others. Paying attention to the needs of others is good for karma, good for the soul, good for the organization, and it starts you on the path of thinking bigger than yourself. It's also a key building block in creating a leader out of you.

Find a strategy that works for you. Answer the question. Make a note to follow up. Put the thing you need to do on your calendar or set a reminder. Respond to the text/message/email/voicemail. Whatever strategy that naturally fits with your style will be easier to turn into a habit. Carve out just a little time for this, the rest can be all about you. Also, call your mother.

Now, let's touch on classic ghosting. The one where you just ignore someone. There is a narrow place where dealing with someone by just not dealing with them is probably the right move. Some guy hounding you by text and he's basically shown you that he's an ass (maybe complete with photos to prove it). Sometimes ignoring someone is the best way to handle it. Trying to tell someone they are being an ass will often end up with them trying to convince you that you are wrong. This is a silly waste of your time and energy. Best to just let it go. Let him go.

But lots of times, we are tempted to disappear on someone, or on a conversation, because it's uncomfortable. We ghost because we don't want to say hard things, hurt people's feelings, or cause people to not like us. All of this is natural. It's easy to just not deal with it, right?

I'll leave this chapter with one ancient piece of advice: How do you want people to treat you, and are you doing the same to them?

Chapter 4: Bad Mouthing

You know this guy? Bob does it in a meeting in front of everyone. "Well, I would have had this ready, but I didn't get what I needed from Carl." Yeah, *that guy*. Many times as a manager, I've had to dig into statements like that. Sometimes it's true. Lots of times it's more complicated, like finding out that Bob didn't follow up with Carl to help make sure it got done. He just sat there and waited for that part to happen, and did nothing to ensure he had what he needed to do his own work and be ready. So he's not blameless here, but…

This is "The Public Bad Mouth." Blaming others for your failure, for a team failure.

Then there's "The Quiet Bad Mouth." Becky strolls over to your workspace and tells you how unfortunate it is that Chelsea didn't do the thing. It's sad, really, she says, because she *likes* Chelsea, but how can she be expected to get her work done when Chelsea didn't do her part?

In my first job out of graduate school, we were doing some coding to get useful research information out of a large database. I was part of the research team, which was full of wonderful, thoughtful people. And then there was the policy team. Full of cocky jackwads. Anyway, my code would be a couple of pages of easy-to-follow and easy-to-validate lines. Then there was John, on the policy team. So cocky. So smug. He would write the same code I did, but would do it in like three lines instead of the 150 I used. And it was probably right, but no one could follow it or check it because it had like 40 nested layers of parentheses. And I complained. To my co-workers, to my boss. To everyone. It was *all* wrong, *see*? John's a cocky jackwad, *see*? He needs to be shamed and then fired. Kicked out of his apartment. I would have said his girlfriend should leave him too, but I assumed no one would date him. Anyway, I might have handled that poorly.

I'll bet you've seen both of these – the public and private bad-mouthing – probably too often. What can you do? A bunch. First, if it happens publicly, don't jump on the train and do it too. And if it's bad enough, maybe grab the target of the bad mouthing after the meeting and ask how you can help. Don't start bad mouthing the source, and don't let yourself get drawn into taking sides. Just ask how you can help, or lend an ear and listen. Remember though, it's entirely possible Chelsea or Carl *didn't* do what was supposed to be done, so this is about empathy for the bad mouthing, not excusing the failure.

If it happens privately, again, don't add to it or encourage the conversation. You can say "Sounds like you need to talk to Carl, let me know how I can help," or something like that.

Then take a minute to look inward. What if it's you doing it? Sometimes you feel like you're defending yourself from blame that shouldn't be yours. You don't want to look bad in front of the boss for something that wasn't your fault. This is a totally legit feeling, so let's talk about *how* to defend yourself without bad mouthing in the process.

"Do you have the project plan ready?"

"Not quite yet. Waiting on one more piece. I'll have it to you by tomorrow."

"Who are you waiting on?"

"Just need to pull the last of the team's contributions together."

In other words, own the delay, and as carefully as you can, say you're waiting on someone without throwing them under the bus. Then go see that person after the meeting and work out getting it done.

If it's a repeat pattern with the person causing your delay, see whether you can work with them to figure out why it's happening and perhaps a way to help. Maybe that person is actually waiting on someone else who isn't doing *their* damn job. If all that fails, then you need to make the tough call to bring it to the boss. But there's usually a kinder, better way to do this; one that does not presume you know *why* it's happening. Keep your focus on the impact to the team effort and that you've tried to help make it better, and now could use some boss help, some boss guidance.

Getting all of this to be a natural part of how you work, managing others and yourself, will help you grow as a human, and as a leader. A big part of doing these things well is empathy. Trying to understand what's driving others and what's affecting them is the key. And it works wonders outside of the office too.

What if it's the boss trashing people? This is a tough one. You have a few options, starting with: Put up with it because you have a good job that you like. Do make sure the scale tips far enough in the "this is *worth* putting up with" direction, however.

If you have a good job, but the boss behavior is too much, you can try to spark some change, or you can leave. Sometimes leaving is absolutely the right answer. And sometimes you just have to realize that work environments and their relationships are imperfect and not always pleasant. Learning the difference will keep you from jumping jobs every time you get irritated or staying in a toxic place too long. There's a balance in there, one that requires a healthy dose of awareness about yourself and others.

If you don't want to put up with it, and you don't want to leave, then going to the boss to talk about the impact of their behavior is my first step. This requires that you are good at these conversations, and that your boss is open to them. This is not a combo that happens often. Be honest with yourself about whether this is a good idea.

Another approach could be in performance-review environments when there are sometimes anonymous surveys of the employees. My last-ditch strategy is going up a level to the next boss. Like talking to your boss directly, this requires a delicate approach, and adds the same need from that boss: To handle it delicately. If they don't, your world could get much worse very quickly. So take the time to think these options through. Don't make decisions rashly here, they are important ones.

Now, what if you're the target of the bad mouth? First, keep calm and don't get defensive. This is easy to say and hard to do. But try. If you hear you're getting trashed behind your back, go to that person and address it directly, and respectfully. "We have some crossed wires here or something, so can we talk and figure out how to move this forward?" Something like that.

And if it's public, it's even harder to keep from being defensive, but try. "Yes, I had some trouble getting this together. I've been working on priorities juggling other things and will catch up with you after the meeting to work through how to get it done." Something. Own it. Don't be defensive, you'll end up looking worse. Figure out a plan for this time. Then start looking at why it happened, whether it's a pattern, and whether you can do anything about it. If you can't see it, or can't fix it, talk to a trusted co-worker, a mentor, a boss if the relationship is good, to help you see what could be a blind spot.

And if you are bad-mouthing people as a strategy to climb higher by stepping on other people, then I offer this: You might very well gain from this, which might reinforce it as a winning tactic. But your reputation and your career will suffer in the long run. Also, this sort of behavior is pretty high up on the list of things that make you an ass. (See Chapter 32, Don't Be an Ass.)

Chapter 5: Do Your Damn Job

My corporate finance mentor was a whirlwind of chaos. She would come bustling into a meeting with stacks of reports and spreadsheets, a giant sippy cup, a calculator, a ruler so she could follow each line in the report correctly, her phone, a laptop, and chaos. I swear you could almost see the kicked-up trail of dust coming in behind her. It was a thing to behold. But she would dive right into it; as deep into the weeds as anyone could ask, and as high level as a C-suiter should be. She could function at any level, efficiently, and quickly. And when we left a meeting, she would go bang out whatever needed to be done. Maybe hit up a few people with questions and then boom, we had a plan, with numbers. Let's roll.

I've had the good fortune to work with an array of talented, capable, dedicated and smart people so far in my career, and I hope you have too. That said...

This chapter shouldn't exist. And yet, here we are.

In my organizational work, I talk to teams and to leadership about what I call "The Low Bar." Over the years, it became depressingly obvious how often people don't do their jobs. It's everywhere. And I don't mean just at the office, but everywhere.

At one point, I noticed that it delighted me when someone actually did their job. I realized then how low my bar had been set. This became "The Low Bar." I don't mean doing a great job, or going above and beyond. No, I mean doing your job at an average level, to meet a reasonable expectation of you doing what you get paid to do.

My doctor's office says they will send the order over to the lab so when I show up to get bloodwork done, the lab is ready for me. And then I show up, and they *are* ready, I am amazed. Or that referral I needed to go see a specialist about some annoying runner injury: They actually sent it over and I scheduled without a hassle. Amazed.

After a meeting, Jesse's task was to put together the takeaways and the next steps. Later that day or the next morning, I would have something waiting for me that was clear, to the point, and useful, and I am astounded. The Low Bar. Because most of the time, I would get nothing for a couple of days, and then maybe, if prompted, some sloppy, lazy, useless pile of nothing would show up. The Low Bar.

When someone says they'll call you tomorrow with an update on something, and they *actually* call you. It's like a little happy gift from above. The Low Bar.

And I am intentionally mixing work and customer service examples. Thinking about your work in terms of customer service is powerful. Whatever you do, you probably have customers. Whether they are actual customers of your organization, or whether they are members of your team, your department, your boss, whatever, think about them, and treat them, as your customers. Making them happy means you are doing your job. This is a simple and effective way to evaluate your own efforts. Are you meeting your customers' needs? Are they happy?

While we're here, I have a couple of important reminders to tuck away in your brain: You're not doing people a favor by doing your job, you are getting paid to do it. You are not being inconvenienced by getting work assigned to you, you are getting paid to do it.

It's one of the biggest hassles to an organization and to everyone else when you don't do your job. This is one of the great challenges of any organization. It's often a sort of invisible bleeding, a low-grade fever.

It usually gets ignored unless it's so bad that it can't be. Why? Managing is hard work. Conflict and criticism are uncomfortable. Firing people is tough.

Hiring new people is tough. It's easier to get by with good enough, right? Here's where I urge you to try the "hard" way. The outcomes are rewarding. If people aren't doing their jobs, when you apply good management and good leadership, it's one of the easiest to control.

And I bet all of you have experienced the hassle of someone not doing their job, something that made your work life or personal life just that much more of a struggle that day. Let's talk about what might be causing it, and what you can do about it.

What causes it? Let's start with that Millennial narrative that we address multiple times in this book, including Chapter 29, The Millennial Excuse. You are lazy, coddled, spoiled, entitled, right? Sure, some of you are, but a lot of this is just a media narrative, a cultural story, we've built up that describes a particular type, not everyone.

One thing worth watching for when you start out at your first job, is that you might not be used to working, all the time, on someone else's schedule, and not being able to do whatever you want. If you were fortunate to grow up where you had those freedoms, then work can seem hard, demanding, the time-suck that takes away from all the fun things, the chill things, that you were doing. Back to this reminder: You are getting paid. It's a job. That makes it on you to get used to it, to do it, and do it well.

Then you've got people who don't really care about the work they do or don't like their job at all. That could be because for a lot of people, their job isn't a career, a profession, their life's calling. It's a job. A paycheck. These people go to work so they can make money to pay for the things they need and want. From paying for basic things like eating and having a roof over their heads, to using their money to do the things that make them happy, all things decidedly *not* in the workplace.

Why does this matter? Because what motivates these people is different than what motivates those who *want* to do the work they are doing. Usually that means setting very clear expectations for attendance, performance, and productivity. Hopefully that's enough. Sometimes, though, you have to use more hands-on management.

And if you're on the same team as this worker-type, but you are not the boss, you have to do the same things to make it go smoothly for you. But you approach it differently, with a peer-to-peer style of engagement, not bossing. This can mean more work for you, because you will have to be more encouraging, check in more, and communicate your needs more. But it's a lot less work than doing your job *and* theirs.

Another reason someone might not be crossing over The Low Bar? A lot of us get stretched too thin. There are roles where the work is *never* done, no matter how much you do. And there are bosses who drive their teams with unrealistic demands and expectations. So that person you are dealing with might love their job but is treading water to keep up with everything.

What can you do? Learn what's going on with that person before you say anything about it. Because if they don't care, that's one approach, but if they do, and are buried, maybe even wracked with guilt for not getting stuff done, then that warrants a very different approach. One that involves extra-gentle care and handling, and often an empathy-driven conversation to see what's going on with them, and working together to figure out how and when you can get what you need. (I tackle the boss angle a bit more in Chapter 9, Managing.)

Maybe that person not doing their job means well and cares, but just isn't that great at managing themselves. This is mostly the same approach as the drowning worker: Find out what's going on before you act on assumptions. Then see how you can help. This is another spot where a little extra work on your part will help get what you need and still be way less work than doing that person's job for them so you can just get your work done. Gentle reminders and check-ins can go a long way with people like this.

We talked a lot here about how to look at – and work with – people who don't clear The Low Bar. Now let's add in an inward look. Is this you? Even a little? You don't want to be that person, so use the same tools, but on yourself. If you don't care all that much about your job, then make sure you remind yourself to do what you are getting paid for. If you are buried, get help. If you have trouble managing yourself, your time, or your workload, find strategies that work for you.

As a manager, I would always push back when people said they would try harder. That's a lousy solution because we're human and we *will* screw up, we *will* drop the ball. I look for approaches that will actually counterbalance whatever someone on my team was struggling with. Forgetting tasks or deadlines? Put them on your calendar. Not a great writer? Get a friend or team member to proofread. Oversleep a lot? Have a buddy call you if he doesn't see your butt at your desk by a certain time. Doesn't matter what they are, just find simple, practical strategies to work with who you are. Those are so much easier than trying to be someone else – to be someone you're not.

Whether in your organization or out in the world with those companies who are taking care of your life maintenance, hold people accountable. Don't do their work for them just to get it done. Work with them when you can to make things right. Definitely speak up.

And if you just can't get them past The Low Bar, find someone else. Go somewhere else. This is an important life skill that comes easily to some people, but for so many of us, it's hard. Really hard. It's worth learning though. A lifetime of not putting up with crap like that will be worth the effort to learn to speak up, to advocate for yourself and your needs.

Make The Low Bar higher, for you, and everyone around you. Start with you. It gives you the room to expect more from others.

Chapter 6: What Are You Worth?

There's a narrative out there that Millennials finish college and expect a starting salary north of $100K, one that goes to a C-suite role and $200K within a couple of years. Even more depending on where they live.

They think they are amazing and should therefore be compensated amazingly. The narrative says they were coddled, told how wonderful they were at every stage, and now have an unrealistic sense of their value. If you have been in the workforce awhile, this can make your eyes twitch.

Of course it's nonsense for most Millennials – and Gen Z now too. They don't feel that way. But just enough of them do to create that narrative and paint all of you with that brush.

Let's break it down into different approaches to make it easier to set your own expectations of what you're worth, and help understand those of the people writing the checks.

Start with what you *need*. You figure out some sort of budget, ranging from super-informal, almost in your head, to a full-blown spreadsheet or app-based thing of beauty. OK, now you know the minimum you need to live, a bit more to be happy maybe, so that's what you need this job to pay you, right? Well, sure, but the job and the boss don't care, and shouldn't have to care, about what you *need* (once you get past the levels in the living wage debate anyway).

What matters is what you are worth to that employer, and what that job is worth. I can't tell you how many times I've interviewed someone and heard what they needed for a salary. Not what they thought the job and their ability to do it were worth, mind you, but what they needed to live the way they wanted to.

A companion piece to what you need, is what you *think* you're worth. People who have been in the workforce longer think they are worth more because they have more tenure and more experience – and hopefully more developed talents and skills. But there's a difference between thinking you're worth more just because you've been around awhile, and actually being worth more because you developed yourself in that time. And it doesn't matter whether you really have become worth more if you are still in a role that isn't worth more.

One way to look at this is in terms of your effect on the organization's bottom line. Not in generalities, but very specifically. And for another way at what a job is worth – to you – break it down by week, or even by day. If you make $52k a year (chosen for easy math), then you can ask yourself this: Was what I did last week worth $1,000? Would I give someone, out of my pocket, $1,000 for this? This is a great way to look at the value of what you're doing, and a useful exercise in realistically assessing what you actually did in a week. Besides eating lunch and checking your email, and dipping into social media, and maybe ordering something online: What did you *do*? Is it worth what you make?

Now let's take this from another angle and look at what the world says your work is worth. Frequently, this isn't fair. Sorry. Take journalists as an example. Lots of them, outside of the big cities, would think that a salary of, say, $50K-$70K a year would be OK. Once you tack on the 15%-30% in taxes and (maybe) benefits that you cost your employer on top of that salary, then a journalist who writes one story a week is saying that story is worth $1,000 to $1,750. And it may very well be, but here's the issue: The rise of the web, the gig economy, and all the freelance talent out there means a penny-pinching boss can get that article written for like $200. So it doesn't matter what you think you're worth and it doesn't matter what you really would be worth in a fair and just world. What matters is what the market *says* you are worth.

It's important to think about classic supply and demand too. Professions that are demanding, difficult, and require extensive preparation or education demand higher salaries. Not many people would go through all the trouble to be doctors, chemists, or engineers if the reward for all the work they put into the training was a low salary. Sure, some would do it purely so they could use the skills to help others, or because it made them happy, but these would be the exceptions, the tails of the bell curve.

On the flip side, all the professions, and the college majors, that are seen as less demanding, true or not, end up with lots more people doing them, because they can't be engineers (yes, I hear you saying you could have, but didn't want to, sure, fine, I know you're the exception, but everyone else...). If you have a huge number of communications or marketing majors competing for a smaller number of jobs, well, those jobs will be harder to get and the salaries will be lower. The point here? Be reasonable in what you expect from what you studied in college, and if it's not enough, then go study something else. Or, get more expertise in your field, go start your own business, or be good enough to rise through your chosen field to be the boss of all things. But you'll have to *do* something.

And while we're here, let's talk about what you can actually *do*. So you majored in communications, great, what can you *do* that will help your employer or prospective employer make more money or serve its customers better? Are you a people person? A great team player? A change agent? Whatever. What can you *do* that is worth someone actually giving you money?

I've met a ton of people who are uncomfortable with this cold, capitalist view. And I get it. These people just want to help, they want to serve, they want to create, they want to make the world a better place. This is all wonderful. But it gets back to supply and demand. There are only so many nonprofits, social service agencies and artistic endeavors that can pay you, and lots of people feel like you do.

With the demand high for these roles and the supply low, especially ones that pay a good salary, it makes it hard to move into these roles. It's unfortunate, but that's just the way it is. Work on yourself to rise to the top of the heap in your skills and abilities so you can compete for these jobs, accept little or no pay for the work, or find something else to do.

Along with salary expectations, people can come right out of college or grad school expecting their feelings of awesomeness to translate to a job that starts near the top of the ladder. The contrast to this, and the friction that it sometimes causes, is an older, traditional sense of "paying your dues" first.

I think there's a balance in there somewhere. A place where you learn and grow; a place where you demonstrate your capabilities and your awesomeness so that you've earned what comes next. This path doesn't require you to be a certain age first, or have a certain amount of time in a role. It *does* require you to spend time proving your value.

If you're trying to answer the question "What is your salary requirement?" (or you are about to ask for a raise because of the great work you're doing, or because your salary doesn't seem to be in line with the industry), do your homework first. For the raise, don't ask for too much in one bump, even when it's warranted. Companies have budgets and bosses can just balk at a big jump. Go for the raise in a couple of steps if it's a big gap to overcome. Whether it's the salary question or a raise, make sure what you expect aligns with your experience, your role, and where the organization is based.

Let's wind this up with three questions for you:

First, over time, are you growing, learning, keeping up, adding new skills, and new strengths? The world doesn't stand still and you can't either.

Second, what value do you bring? What work do you do that helps the mission? How much handholding, babysitting and deadline extensions do you need? If your boss has a project, can she give you a problem, some general guidance, a deadline, and send you off to make it happen? Can she have confidence that it will actually happen?

Third, what does your boss *think* you're worth? What do you do to make her job easier, smoother, more effective? How do you help him move the organization's mission forward?

You want to be worth more? Here it is in a nutshell: Do your job, do it well, do it on time, take initiative, figure things out on your own. Be a good team player. Grow. Build up others. Make your boss look good. Make her job easier. Anticipate what needs to be done, don't wait to be told.

What are you *really* worth?

Chapter 7: Communication

How many times have you been in a meeting – virtual or not – and just zoned out, or worked on something else? How about for a conference call, reading through a long email, a report, or a proposal?

There are lots of reasons for this, and if we ignore the ones that involve you not getting enough sleep the night before because of some questionable use of your time, a lot of it will come down to relevance and communication.

Relevance here centers on the notion that what's interesting or important to you will hold your attention better. Using this simple idea can help you hold the attention you need from others. And it can help you figure out how to stay engaged when the topic is not as relevant to you as something else that's going on, but it's important enough to your job or your relationships that it's worth paying attention.

Even when an idea is interesting or at least important, if it's poorly communicated, it is still likely to miss the landing with your audience. When a meeting, report, email, conference call, proposal, is too long, takes too long to get to the point, wanders around different points – well, you get the idea – we lose interest, we get bored, or irritated, or lost.

This chapter is trying to cover such an incredibly wide array of methods and modes that I am taking a deep breath, moving fast, and not looking at any one piece right in the eye lest it grab me and insist on a full deep dive. Nobody's got time for that...

Each form of communication has rules to do it well. Some of them carry across different forms, some don't.

Let's start with five things you should pay attention to, because if you do these well, you will be rewarded:

1. Learn to write a complete sentence. Learn to write, period. This matters a lot, across nearly all professions. And if you *can* write, but don't because you've gotten used to communicating in messaging-platform format across everything you do, well, stop it. Think about when highly abbreviated, acronym-laden communication makes sense, and when it really doesn't. Don't use "r u" at work when you should use "are you." Easy enough, right?
2. Play to your strengths. Are you better with spoken word or written? Is the topic better suited for something in writing, a meeting, or quick conversation in an office, or even in the hall? This is one of those many things that is not "one size fits all." Much of how I communicate does not always translate well in writing. I imagine I am trying to be clever or funny, and in writing, it's sometimes either confusing or off-putting. I've had to learn many lessons the hard way over the years to edit myself depending on context, (See Chapter 17, Be You, Just Less). Play to your audience's strengths too (communicate for them too, not just for you). Are you dealing with engineer types who appreciate lots of detail and logically thought-out communication? Are you dealing with that boss who has the attention span of a toddler and will seize on some key word and go with it? Knowing these things in advance and accommodating them will save you a lot of headache.
3. Be brief. Be ruthless in your own editing. Whatever you write or say should be only as long as it needs to be to communicate effectively; no more, no less. This is just as important when you are talking with an individual, or a group, as it is in writing.
4. Take the time to think, review, edit, look up things, double-check. Otherwise you will look ignorant, lazy, sloppy, dumb. A good reminder is that spell check will save you, over and over, and you should use it. A related reminder is that it will catch a typo, but usually not the *wrong* word. Sometimes the features that check style and usage will help, but a lot of this is on you. Also, taking the time to put something down and come back to it later is always a good

idea, especially when you are irritated, angry, or in a hurry. Toning down or deleting your own scathing communication will serve you well. And when it comes to spontaneous spoken communication (as opposed to planned presentations that you can practice), remember to be nice, be brief, get to the point, and then hush.

5. Watch clichés, buzzwords, and jargon. Don't be the guy who says "synergy" or the girl who says "parking lot," or whatever overused thing is trending. Do you really want to be the one that lets them complete their buzzword bingo card? Jargon is often overused by newbies trying to sound knowledgeable or smart, but it comes off as silly most of the time. More senior people, including leaders, might use jargon to exclude "outsiders," or to intimidate or dominate the newer members of the team. Watch for those negative motivations in your use of language. Stick to the jargon that's truly relevant to your profession and avoid the rest, especially the overused ones that are thrown out to avoid action. "Let's take that offline." "Let's put a pin in that." "Let's put that in the parking lot." Those all can be useful to keep a meeting focused, but when you use them to avoid saying, "Yeah, we're not going to do that," it will show. You come off like that parent who says "We'll see," or "Let me talk to your mother," or "Let me think about it." Those became a running joke in my house because my kids would say, "So, no then?" because they knew it meant no. If you say something needs to "Go in the parking lot," or something like it, it's incumbent on you to follow up and address that issue. This is the right way to do it, and it will mean a lot to the people on your team.

These five ideas will serve you well in general, but when you are working on something that's important to you or your boss, take the time to hit the web for best-practices ideas. I usually can find one or two easy changes that make my work better. Lots of data? Create good visuals. Need to build a PowerPoint deck? Keep the content on each slide to one thought, maybe two. Illustrate your points where it makes sense. A report to do? Try this: Write a title that conveys the point. A summary paragraph that does it better, a full page that really covers it all, and then add whatever supplementary materials your readers might need for reference. Now does it have to be one page? No, but like a resume, if it's going to be longer, it had better be worth it.

When you are giving a presentation: Don't read line for line whatever's on the screen. They can read; it's insulting and a waste of time. Talk to your audience. Just talk to them. And if you have a time limit, don't exceed it, just don't. Better yet, come in under the wire. People will love you for it. And if there isn't a time limit, decide what makes sense for your audience, your organizational culture, and stick to it. One guide that I use all the time is that most of the videos I see aren't more than about three minutes. Yours doesn't need to be that short, but the longer it is, the more you risk losing people. Keep it tight; keep it focused.

And just as reviewing and editing your own work is critical, practicing that presentation is too. If you think it's three minutes and it's really 10, well, that's bad. Practice it, time it, and then be ruthless cutting and tightening. And don't wing it. You might think you are that good, but you probably aren't. Practice is not weakness, it's polishing, it's smart, and it shows respect for your audience. And if you can talk someone into putting up with you, practice in front of a human. Get feedback, and listen to it.

A key aspect of communication is that nobody knows how you feel, what you think, what you mean, what you believe. They only know what you say and what you do. I read something long ago that stuck with me likening this to a train tunnel. What you know about your thinking is on one end and all full of light and sunshine, and what everyone else knows about what's in your head is that little tiny dot of light at the end of the tunnel. You have it all, but they only see a tiny bit of insight into your brain. Getting the communication right can mean everything.

Since so much of what we do these days is written in some form, it's worth talking about the pitfalls to avoid. It's probably happened to all of you where something you wrote either came across with an entirely different meaning than you intended, or the meaning was clear, but it still landed poorly. Think about all that the written word lacks, and this is no surprise. Body language, facial expressions, and voice tone can all carry a huge amount of information, of nuance. My first solution to this was to be exceptionally clear and detailed in whatever I wrote. Turns out that doesn't work for everyone. It makes what you write very long, and without the tone, can come across as lecturing or bossy or patronizing. As I worked over the years to become more and more concise, I also had to practice getting the meaning right, practice being very clear, without screwing it up in these other ways.

Getting this right is worth your time. Between email, reports, messaging and collaboration platforms, hell, even texting, we write so much of what we communicate. It's almost a given that any job description, no matter how technical, will probably say something about "excellent interpersonal and communication skills," because if you miss the mark here, the rest might not matter.

Whether you are in a meeting, or a one-on-one, a simple, and amazingly effective, edit to a common phrase will improve the outcome of these interactions. "Are there any questions?" You hear it all the time. There usually aren't any. Change it to this: "Tell me what questions you have?" Be OK with some silence. Sometimes I'll belt out "I LOVE AWKWARD PAUSES," in a goober effort to break the tension, then I wait even longer. Someone has something to say. Help them do it.

This is an example of an open-ended question. They are wonderful. "How are you doing?" often gets you a one-word answer. "What's going on with you?" or "Tell me about your day," almost always gets a whole lot more.

Let's tie it together with this: Know your audience. Some people want to watch a video, some people want to read something. Some people love all sorts of detail, some people only want the highlights. Take the time to understand *who* you are trying to reach and accommodate them.

If you're a storyteller, and lots of people are, be careful with length, style, and placement. We see a lot of guidance about "humanizing" or "personalizing" our communications. What does that better than leading off with a story?

I got an email newsletter from a local nonprofit that does important work in my community. It started with a personal story from the CEO about something meaningful and impactful in her life, then she tied that into what was going on in the community, then closed by essentially saying "Keep reading for all that's going on in our organization." Sounds perfect, right?

But here's where she missed a chance to communicate effectively: First, her story was all about her. Even though she tied it in to the point, it went on and on about her – and her obviously amazing depth and intellect. We let ego get in the way sometimes because we like to talk about ourselves. After all, we're experts about our lives, and we're awesome, right?

Second, she went on too long with the story. By the time I got to all the updates and happenings, they had almost lost my attention. It's not a good idea to spend a lot of readers' time on something that isn't the main point. You've exhausted their attention by the time you get to the reason you're there.

Third, when your communication style and storytelling is highly detailed, long, expansive, and full of feelings, you end up reaching about half the audience. All the rest who wanted something factual, brief, and to the point were forced to wade through content, length, and style that didn't work for them.

It's easy to think being detailed and full of feelings is the right way to communicate, but it's a form of bias in that it's the way you think and shouldn't be attributed to everyone. It's just as easy to think that everyone will appreciate a short, facts-only approach too. That's simply bias in the other direction.

Knowing your audience will help you be more effective because you either send more than one style of communication, or if it's just one version going to everyone, you work to find a happy medium between long storytelling and get-to-the-point facts. If you find that balance, you have a better shot at reaching everyone.

OK, enough of all this, you get the idea. But as we close here, I want to emphasize this big-picture point: One of the most powerful and effective ways to communicate is to be brief, to be accurate, and to choose your words thoughtfully. No matter the type of work you do, these are skills that will serve you well, and are worth your attention and your time.

Chapter 8: Meetings

Good grief, where to start? No one likes meetings. No one. Well, except you, Carol. You like spending time together and going over *everything*. And you, Jacob. You like to get out of working and basically goof off during the whole meeting. You two both go sit in a corner and think about your behaviors. Anyway, for the rest of us, we don't like meetings.

There is so much written about them: About how bad they are, how much time they waste. The day before I sat down to write this chapter, there was yet another piece on them, this one about how the more you meet, the fewer creative ideas you come up with. With all that baggage, that negativity, that bleak reputation, why bother at all?

Let's take this in two parts: The first is an argument that some topics lend themselves to meetings. The second part is that a well-run meeting is night-and-day different from most of the others.

For topics: The subtleties matter. Let's say there's a new project to introduce to the team and get it going. If it's a routine project, then an email, or a conversation in a collaboration platform like Slack or Teams is usually plenty, and often, even better. But let's say the new project is huge or different or extra complicated. Then a brief meeting can be a great tool. Get everyone together, lay out briefly what the new thing is, tell everyone all the supporting materials are coming to them in their collaboration platform, and then take the time to seek feedback, concerns, questions. This is key and has to be done by a leader who knows what she's doing. Go around the room, tell people what they will be responsible for, what they need to start with, what you need them to report back on first. Then seek first impressions, challenges, opportunities, whatever they are. Make sure everyone knows that it's OK to say, "Everything seems good to me, let's get started." In other words, create an environment where it's just fine to *not* have anything to add.

The second part is about a well-run meeting. If you call meetings or lead meetings, here's what we all need from you:

- Be brief and to the point
- Ensure the topic is relevant to the people you've invited
- Keep people focused, and the discussion on-point
- Actually seek and listen to input from the people in the room
- Make meetings short and infrequent
- Get stuff done.

You probably see the pattern here: It's the stuff that usually doesn't happen in the world of meetings. If you do all of these things, people will start to see the value, the efficiency in the meetings you *do* have, and appreciate you and the workplace culture for all the ones you don't.

Two more ideas for those who call the meetings: Be wary of standing meetings, except one-on-ones (and I advocate passionately for those). Standing meetings tend to be more about reporting what's happened already, and what routine things are upcoming. Anything that can be done in advance – with a report, any sort of update, instructions, guidance, additional information, and so on – absolutely do that in advance and not in a meeting. If you really want a standing meeting, a staff meeting, literally make them where people are gathered and standing, and for no more than about 10 minutes.

Second, don't be selfish and self-centered as a boss. Everyone's time matters too, not just yours. We've probably all been in meetings that were called with little or no notice, or at a time that really interrupted whatever was going on. Be the team player who thinks about others. This is hard for bosses, because they often treat everyone as tools to help the boss get his job done. This often comes off as uncaring, imperious, and selfish.

The wrinkle here is that the boss's team *is* actually there to help the boss get her job done (well, really, the boss and everyone else is there to accomplish the mission, but you know what I mean). The key though is to think about everyone else's time, workload, and schedule, when summoning them all for a meeting. It's easy to think of your own time as a boss as so much more valuable than everyone else's, and in some ways it is, but find that balance. If you come in at 7 every morning because that's when you're done at the gym, don't schedule meetings at 7 when everyone else comes in at 8 or 9. Not cool. Same with scheduling at lunch time, late in the day, weekends, or evening. All of those windows need to be used sometimes, but when people see the scheduling was for the right reasons, that it was really needed, then the fact that it sucks can be a shared experience for everyone, including the boss.

If you're wondering what's wrong with all of those other bosses, because *your* meetings are great and people love them, well, maybe you can help those other bosses by sharing these things to watch for, these symptoms of bad meetings:

- People fidgeting or not paying attention
- If a recurring meeting, people finding reasons to miss them
- No one has any input
- Nothing useful gets done
- They take longer than needed or run over allotted time
- Meeting not controlled, people and topics not kept focused.

Now let's turn the coin over. If you are summoned to meetings, here's what everyone needs from you:

- Show up
- Be on time
- Be prepared
- Be brief
- Don't say something someone else already did just because you think so highly of your version of the same words. Don't be that guy. Especially if a woman already said it. Double penalty points for being *that* guy in two lousy ways.

- Stay on point and out of the weeds
- If something should be discussed after the meeting, do that. Don't waste everyone's time with how this project interferes with your weekend plans or some other item that's hyper-focused on you
- Be positive
- Don't dominate
- Pay attention. This may be the hardest one. As so many meetings moved to Zoom, the format laid bare a lot of what's been going on all along. We can see people looking at their monitors doing something else. And we know most of the camera-off people are not paying attention. Hell, half of those people probably aren't even sitting there.

Diving a bit more into how you behave at a meeting: Are you fidgety and whiny about it all? This makes you look like a toddler. Seriously, you're a grown-up, you can sit still for an hour of something boring. It's good life practice. Are you catty and snarky with your neighbor, making fun of the meeting and the people in it through whispers or messages? Congratulations, you've graduated from toddler to teenager.

As adults, we should be able to handle this with grace and class, because we are adults. Not everything about work is fun, right? And most of us are not at the top of the food chain calling the shots. Being confident that you can and would do it better is great motivation to move up the chain and have more influence, or to strike out on your own, or maybe to join a very small and informal organization. But until then, you are playing in someone else's sandbox and need to live by their rules.

We are learning more about "neurodiversity" and people who are "neuro-atypical" every year, and like many other things in this book, how people think – how their brains actually work – varies across a spectrum. It's possible, for example, your fidgets are from a genuine trouble sitting still for a long while. For me, it comes down to a few key ideas to help with this: Keep your meetings infrequent and short, and figure out the best ways to communicate and interact with each person. And if it's you who struggles with some of the traditional formats of work life, look for ways to make them work for you.

A big change in the world of meetings came out of the pandemic. So many meetings became virtual, but there's another wrinkle to the story: A lot of the meetings aren't really traditional meetings, they are collaborative work sessions. The biggest difference is it's OK for silence. Really. People are just working together and can talk when it's relevant. And these work-session meetings might not have a leader. These changes require a bit of mindset shift and help you expand how you look at – and approach – meetings.

Chapter 9: Managing

One of my favorite movies about managing is the cult classic "Office Space." If you know anyone who is partial to a red Swingline stapler, that's why. There is plenty of lousy managing going on in that movie, a lot of behaviors from what I call "anti-role models." For me, anti-role models are just as important as role models. Looking in the mirror to ensure you are not doing something you don't like when you see it in others is just as powerful as working to emulate traits in others that you appreciate.

Let's dive right in with a few typical problems. The first is that managing is a job all by itself, and it is often not treated that way. So many times, a new manager is expected to keep doing the job she already had in addition to now taking care of a team.

The second is that people who are good at their jobs often get promoted with a widely held *assumption* that they also will be good managers. This is as much nonsense as saying a star athlete will make a great coach. She might, but not just because she was a star.

Third, we often do very little to support and train new managers. Mostly, it's "Here's your new title, good luck, don't screw it up."

And finally, it's the key internal question; a sort of existential one: Do you actually *want* to be a manager? Or do you just think you should because it's how career advancement works? I ask this one because managing is work, hard work. And it might not be all that rewarding for you. If it's not, look to be a rock star in the work you do, not in management. Sometimes that requires moving to an organization that understands management is not an automatic, or the only, career path. And it's not the only measure of success.

Knowing these four potential troubles, let me add this: If you are in a leadership role, don't cause them for new managers, and if you're that new manager, know that the deck is stacked against you a little and cut yourself a break. Then do the work to make yourself a good manager.

I equate managing to conducting a symphony or directing a show: You are not playing an instrument. You are not in front of the camera acting. You are making it all happen, and the better you do it, the happier and more productive everyone is, and the more successful your organization is in its mission.

When you become a manager, it can be hard to give up the work you do because, well, it's what you do. It can be hard to give up because you might actually *like* doing it, and sometimes because you feel like, or are made to feel like, that if you aren't *doing* the work, you aren't doing anything of value. This is piffle. (I really wanted to use "piffle" in this book somewhere, so just let me have this one.)

There's a good argument for sometimes jumping in and doing the work, not just managing it. The idea is to make sure you know what your team is dealing with; and to keep up with changes and trends as your work evolves. The reasons are sound, but the key here is *sometimes*. Of course, jumping in to do the work in an emergency is a different case, and one that is often helpful to the mission, and shows the team that you are right there with them dealing with whatever is happening.

If you're already a manager or plan to be soon, here are some tips:

- "Don't borrow tomorrow's problems." This is a saying from a mentor of mine. It's simple, but it's a good reminder that you can very quickly get stuck on "what-if" scenarios when you are trying to make something happen. Deal with what's in front of you, and anticipate the most likely things to happen, not every last little weird thing that might happen.
- "Don't boil the ocean" was another wonderful saying of that mentor. Work on what you can. Work on each piece as it comes. Solve the

first step. Don't try to plan it all out and fix the whole world in one shot. You'll get stuck and do nothing.

- Ask yourself regularly: What problem am I trying to solve? This is one of my favorite coaching tools. I ask it a lot. It's a great way to focus the agenda; to focus your thinking and your questions. And if you don't have the answer, or your team doesn't, then that's likely the problem you should start with.
- The cliché boss saying "Bring me solutions, not problems" is a dated concept and should be avoided. If your team had all the answers, they wouldn't be coming to you. When they have an issue, encourage them to think through it, and to bring possible solutions, but don't mandate them. Help them work through it; help them come up with solutions.
- In Chapter 19, Hard Things and Scary Things, I dig into another favorite coaching tool of mine: What is the cost of being wrong? This is a great guide for making decisions, and for how much time you spend on each one.
- Know that different people respond to different styles of managing. You can be mostly or totally hands-off with some, in the middle with others, and there are always a few who really need a lot of guidance on a regular basis. On top of that, people respond differently to being managed. Some need a firm hand; some respond well to more gentle coaching. I am absolutely advocating an approach that is not "one-size-fits-all." It's easy to fall into a trap of expecting everyone to just put up with how you manage because you're the boss. You can do it that way, but you won't be a good one.
- Don't fall into the trap of ignoring your solid team members. We end up devoting all our time to the problem people and because of that triage, tend to ignore the ones who should be getting your attention too, just for better reasons.
- Too many new managers are afraid to let others do the work they were doing, or are afraid to explain or teach what they do. It comes from an insecurity that the company won't need them anymore. And

> it can come from a fear that others will screw it up. You have to fight these urges when they strike. You can't manage well without teaching and helping others develop. You can't manage well without using your new team to free up some of your time for use at a higher level than task performance.

You manage your team, but you also manage your peers and your boss. Managing your peers is done with good reasoning and good arguments, and by having solid working relationships with them. If you burn people or climb over them to get ahead, you can guess how it's going to go when you need something from them.

"Managing up." That's how I look at dealing with your boss. We get so focused on managing our team, we tend to think about being managed *by* our bosses. But knowing how they want information, for example, in what detail, and when, will make things go much more smoothly for you. It's a great way to make the team you are part of work more smoothly: Know how to talk to your boss in her language. Know what she wants and how you can help her be effective in her role.

I've had bosses who wanted two-sentence summaries of just about anything. And I've had bosses who wanted every last bit of supporting detail. Avoid the trap of talking to your boss the way that works well for *you*, not the way *she* wants to get information. Same with being in the loop. Some bosses want a little, some want every last detail. Figure out what yours wants and do it that way.

A good idea to remember about managing your boss: Be careful how you phrase things you bring to them. When you tell your boss about something that is not going well, or you suggest something be done differently, they can hear it as criticism. They can hear you saying, whether you mean to or not, whether it's true or not, that you think they are not doing it right.

This is irritating to lots of bosses and can cause defensive reactions that won't go well for you. Watch your word choice here. A little extra care can go a long way. "Hey boss, I like how we are doing X, but I was thinking about trying Y, what do you think? Worth a try?" Or, "Hey boss, that important thing got screwed up. Is it OK if I dig into what happened to see how we can fix it and prevent it in the future?"

Let's go back to you as a manager: Make sure your expectations are reasonable. People need a life outside of the office and they need you to not wear them out. Especially if it feels like a selfish thing because you are just doing whatever *your* boss wants and not pushing back to protect your team from unreasonable demands and deadlines.

Sometimes you *do* have to demand a lot, so make sure this is the exception, not the rule. Show real empathy for what you're asking, and work with them on ways to make it happen and minimize the pain. This is often a good time to get down in the trenches with them, work alongside them, and put in the hours they do.

Let's wrap up with two big traps: Shiny Things and Doing It All Your Damn Self.

Are you the manager or leader who has no attention span, no ability to plan, to focus on details? Great, let's throw out all traditional project planning and work structures, and just be "lean," "nimble," or "agile." Let's act like we are a "start-up" all the time regardless of how long we've been around.

These latest fads or trends are attractive as excuses for those who just want to do and not think or plan. Don't get me wrong, there's a time and a place for these styles. But make sure it's not just so you can avoid doing work you don't like. If you're an "idea" person who loves to just make it go, then instead of ignoring all the work that can make you more successful at it, make sure you have that person on your team who thrives on the details and who will likely save your butt regularly. And appreciate them for what they bring.

The other trap, especially for new managers, is to just do it yourself. Uncomfortable asking someone to do some work? Oh, just do it yourself. Do you think it will take longer to explain than to do it? Just do it yourself. Are you convinced that Becky will screw it up; that Larry will take a week to do something that will take you a day? Just do it yourself. Afraid they won't need you anymore if others are doing the work? Just hang on to the knowledge and do it yourself.

There are plenty of reasons managers do this, but they all come at a cost. If you use your team, you can do more than you can do solo. If you spend the time to teach them, the investment will pay off once they get it. You leverage all of their time into so much more than you can do yourself. Plus, you will make people feel valued and needed, one of the hallmarks of a good manager, and a key to keeping those on your team from jumping ship for something better.

If you *really* believe they can't do it, and you have genuinely tried to get them there – and haven't avoided the difficult and candid conversations – then you have another important management challenge: being strong enough to replace people; strong enough to make sure you have the right people, not just making do with who you have. This is one of the things that sets good managers apart from the rest.

Chapter 10: Leading

Ask yourself *why* you want to lead. Actually, first ask yourself *whether* you want to lead at all.

If the answer is "no," that's OK. Really.

Don't get caught up in the conventional wisdom that it's the only path. It's not. Being amazing at your job can be powerfully fulfilling, and the right path, for a lot of people. The key is to be in an organization that values expertise as much as it values leadership. If not, find another one, or fly solo if that suits you.

If you *do* want to lead, then why? If it's just to be a big shot, well, that's a different conversation. If it's truly to make things better, to lead the team, to conduct the "musicians" in performing something wonderful, then you're in the right frame of mind to build your leadership skills.

You can be a great leader, and maybe not so good as a manager (which is more about managing people and processes). You can be a great manager, and a lousy leader. Or maybe you are just beginning in your career and need to develop skills all-around. These scenarios all have solutions.

A good leader is aware of her strengths and weaknesses, and surrounds herself with people who make the whole better. I've known plenty of strong leaders who also needed a strong right-hand person to manage everything.

And if you are a great manager and not a great leader? Take that important bit of self-awareness and either decide that management is your thing and be a leader's right hand, or start working on those weaknesses so you can lead well too.

I talked about awareness in the Introduction to this book but bring it up here again because it's crucial to becoming a successful leader. You can't do much to make you better if you are trying to fix the wrong things, or conveniently ignoring the ones that need the most work, or, my favorite, you don't think you have anything to work on.

There are shelves upon shelves of books about leadership, so let's narrow it down to a few key concepts that can make all the difference.

The first is to put your people first. Something I learned in the Marine Corps and have carried with me forever: A good sergeant gets in at the end of the chow line. This is meant literally, and as a metaphor for putting your team first. You take the hit, not them. You suffer, not them. Give others the credit, you take the blame. Your job is to make them work well together, to understand the mission and to carry it out well. If you are a selfish jerk who just wants to climb the ladder or make money, it will show.

Next, put the mission first, not the metrics. This one can be tough with so much focus on profits and on maximizing shareholder value. (Side note: If you think profits are dirty, and you are working in a for-profit environment, then the problem is you, not them, and you are working in the wrong place.) If you focus, for example, only on profits (the metric), it might work short term, but it will not be healthy in the long term. If you focus on delivering a quality product or service, and leading a lean and high-functioning team, then it will show in your bottom line. (See Chapter 65, It's Measure, Not a Target.) The strength it takes to balance these competing demands is a test of leadership.

Now think about *how* to lead. Think about how to connect with your team, and to connect them to each other. Think about motivating them, inspiring them; getting them to see the shared objectives.

Define the problem or the goal. Why is it important to the company, to you, and why should it be important to them? And not getting fired does not count as motivation or the reason it's important.

When working with organizations: I ask "Who are you?" "Where are you going?" and "How are you going to get there?" And I keep pushing on this with the leadership team until everyone is happy with the answers. Only then can you move forward effectively.

Take these three questions and first answer them for yourself as a leader. This is personal development, a focus on you, that can bring clarity to your path.

Then take the same questions and make sure you can answer them for your organization, for the mission in front of you, and for your team. Leading well starts with your ability to articulate the vision.

Leadership can be hard, it can be scary, and it can be lonely. That's one reason you need mentors at every level, and it's a reason why having a peer group to connect with can be powerful.

And stop trying to be their buddy. The best leaders have real empathy, real understanding and caring about their people, but at the same time, they must be firm and make tough decisions that might be unpopular.

If you want to go that route, to become a leader, you have to start growing in that direction. This means getting mentors, and using the time they give to learn and develop yourself. Look for projects to take on where you can lead, even informally. When you display leadership qualities, people will gravitate to you. And to me, one of the purest forms of leadership is earned, not conferred. If you can get a team of peers that doesn't *have* to listen to you to listen to you, and be willing to do it a second time, then you've done well.

And work on yourself. Be intentional about it. There's no silver bullet, no magic pill. No MBA or other training alone will do it. It also takes time, experience, judgment, self-awareness, growth – it takes a lot of things working together to shape you.

There's a term lots of you might see called "WIP," or Work In Progress, as a status of an item or a project. I am my own lifelong WIP. My goal is to be better this year than last year. Every single year. You should take this on too. (For you, not me. I already have people in my life who will tell me, unasked, how to do everything better or at least that I am doing it all wrong.) Read a book on leadership. Take an online class. Listen to some podcasts. Close your mouth, and open your eyes and ears to how others lead.

This is about all the things that go into making you a great leader. It's about listening. It's about judgment, maturity, empathy, and decisiveness. It's about a lot of qualities, and when you see the good ones in leaders, look at yourself in the mirror and see where you need work. Then go do it. If it was easy, anyone could do it.

Look at leaders around you, not just in a workplace context, but everywhere. Start making a short list of the traits you admire and want to emulate. Just as important, make a list of what the jackass leaders do. Even if you are not the person who would generally be a jackass, if you're not paying close attention to you, and to how others are reacting to you, then it's easy to end up with some of those lousy traits.

Too often in the organizational work I do I see C-Suite leaders who specialize in making the CEO happy and generally trying to look good. A happy CEO should be an outcome of your – and your team's – great work, not the thing you spend your day spinning a magical narrative about.

Ask yourself whether you are truly leading, or are you just trying to look good to your boss and get promoted by doing whatever he says, whatever makes him happy? Do you push back?

In the opposite direction, do you try to be one of your team, have them all like you and blame everything unpleasant on "corporate" or "higher-ups" or something? You *do* need to look out for your team, advocate for them and champion their work, but you are not their buddy. The responsibility for the pain and stress in their work lives rests with you, even if it doesn't start with you.

True leadership is hard. You have to balance making your people happy, your boss happy, and your need to be happy and healthy too. You represent the organization and its mission, not just yourself or your area of ownership. Leadership is not for everyone and is not easy, automatic, or something that can be set on autopilot. Like any relationship, it takes effort, care, and focus.

Chapter 11: Do What You Say

I remember having a drink with my dad after I turned 21. He was talking to me like I was an actual grown-up, so it's a memory that stuck. And something he said that day resonated with me, and still does. He spent 20+ years as an officer in the Marine Corps and was still a young man in his 40s when he "retired" from the military. He was working in a medium-sized company in the corporate world and shared this: "Boy," he said, "something I'll never understand. When I ask people to do something, sometimes they just don't."

You see, for a Marine officer, that's not a thing you would experience very often. And in my view, it should be an exception when any of us experience it. But we all know it's not.

We got at some of this in the chapters on ghosting and doing your job, but this one is so important, it needs its own chapter.

Too often, we focus on what we need to do, what's important to us, what our priorities are. When what's top of mind is ourselves, then a common side-effect of that is we just blow off, procrastinate, or forget, things that other people are waiting for. Things they are counting on us for.

I have one piece of advice, and it will be short: Cut it out.

There's an old saying most of us know as "The Golden Rule" that advises to "do unto others as you would have them do unto you."

When you need that report, that update, that whatever, so you can move forward in your work, and they just don't do it, and often don't even bother with an excuse, how does it feel? How does it affect you?

There's a reason that old-school cable TV companies were the butt of so many jokes: Their installer track record was terrible. They'd basically show up, or not, whenever they got to it, regardless of whether you had a "window," and frankly, you were lucky to even get a window. Maybe you had that experience with a tech for your internet install, or maybe a repair person who was going to come fix something at your home. This stuff is irritating at best, and at worst it affects our ability to be successful in whatever we're doing. And you know this is true, so why on Earth would you do it to someone else?

After reading this, if you looked in the mirror and saw a guilty face, all you need to do is to *do* something about it. If you don't have a good system to stay on top of things, start there. Some ideas are really simple, but they work. Anything I need to do ends up on my calendar. I live by the stupid thing. But it works. If I get off a call or out of a meeting, and I have a to-do, I either do it right then, put it on the daily working list I use, or put it on my calendar for when I will do it. This might not work for you, and that's fine. I'm just saying to find a strategy to manage you in a way that works for you.

The old saying "underpromise and overdeliver" says a lot. Be careful that you don't get carried away in the excitement of it all and commit to more than you can handle. And don't overcommit because you're in the spotlight and the boss is looking at you. These on-the-spot situations can lead to acting quickly without thinking or even because you're a little panicky. Know what you can manage. Even when that means you have to stretch, there's still a limit.

And if you're a selfish piece of work, well, that's gonna take a little more effort. But if you tackle that one, your life in and out of work will be so much better for the one who matters most to you: You. The fact that everyone else is happier is a bonus for them, but how they interact with you and how your life goes will be smoother. For you. See where I'm going with this? Win-Win even if you only think about the first "win."

Changing gears now: If it happens to you – someone promises and doesn't deliver – start taking steps to demand better. Out in the world, when someone doesn't do what they say, I "fire" them and find someone else. I'm not an ass about it, but I am clear as to why. And if you can't fire someone, like the tech coming to fix your cable modem, you can damn sure complain, and you should. This stuff matters and if you don't just let it go, things often get better.

In the office, again, don't be an ass, but talk to people directly. A hard lesson I learned is to find out what happened before you take the next steps. More than once I pushed hard on someone only to find that they had a really good reason, an emergency or something. You look like, and are, a jerk for dumping on someone who didn't get you whatever it was they should have, but was in the hospital after getting sideswiped on their bike by a car. Always ask first.

But once you politely assess, that no, he just didn't do it, then have that talk. And if it doesn't work, say something like, "OK, let's get with your boss to talk about my expectations. I want to make sure I'm not off-base here," or something careful like that. But don't let it go. It won't be the last time.

One last strategy? If it's family or your boss, or someone or something else that you really can't control or sometimes even say anything to, then take steps to protect yourself. Plan for their failure and be surprised and happy when they don't. For example, if I have to wait for someone to show up between 8 and noon, I don't schedule anything that I can't move the rest of that day. In other words, build in buffer time. If you rot in the doctor's office for an hour before she sees you, don't let that make you miss a meeting. Plan to be there the extra hour. Plan to use the time effectively while you wait. You get the idea. Have a plan. Then have a backup plan.

A pro-tip for reading this far: Whenever you can, especially with bosses, ask them for things that have a course of action spelled out if they DON'T say anything. I was talking with someone who was managing the logistics for a large board of directors. She basically said she spent half her week trying to get lunch selections from 40 very (self-)important people. And she definitely had much better things to do with her time. My suggestion: Very sweetly say, here are your lunch choices. Let me know what you want by Friday. If I don't hear from you, you get the chicken.

Same thing for work. "Hey boss, here's what I plan to do on that action item, let me know if you want something different. Otherwise, I'll have at it." This is a very powerful tool, just be careful to be very clear about this. Don't be a weasel and bury it at the bottom of some long thing so you get the outcome you want when your boss misses it. That will burn you. Also, don't be a weasel is good advice all around.

And sometimes we get overcommitted by our families, by our bosses, by ourselves. We're not bad people, we are just buried. The outcome is the same though, and it's still on us to make it happen. There are lots of places in this book to help with your priorities, with managing you. But it's up to you to get there. To get to a place where you do what you say.

Chapter 12: Workplace Love

You have probably experienced, maybe firsthand, what happens when a relationship at work goes badly. If that's not enough of a lesson on why these should be avoided, then let's keep going.

It's easy to say "Avoid relationships," but so much harder to do. The "why" it happens is simple: We spend a lot of time with people at work. Often they look their best too, so that doesn't hurt. Any environment where people spend time together, friendships grow. Romances blossom. And for many of us, that's the only place where we see a lot of people and spend time with a lot of people. We get to know them in a safe and comfortable way that's nothing like trying to go to a bar to connect with a stranger.

Since I am confident this chapter will fail in its large mission to convince you to avoid workplace relationships entirely, because "love is blind" – and dumb and stupid – I do hold out hope that you can minimize the damage to you and to those around you.

Start with a super-obvious one, but it's the most important: No dating anyone you manage or who manages you. Most companies explicitly forbid it, but even if they don't, this is a recipe for disaster. And if you're ever tempted, or your boss is, ask yourself this before you even think about the next step: Am I willing to quit this job to go on a date? If the answer is no, then you have your answer.

And when one of you says you can just keep it a secret, on the down-low: Make sure you understand that you're hiding it because it's wrong. Are you OK with what that says about you? Also understand that no matter how clever you think you are, people will find out.

If you must date someone at work, then the more removed from your area, the better. Beyond not dating in your line of supervision, it's healthy to keep it outside of your department or area. Even when he is outside your area, when she is not in your department, think through how it will be if it ends badly. Will you dread going to work? I know it's hard to think through much of anything rational and logical in the beginning, but try. Try to imagine how your life will be if this plays out in some of the typical ways relationships do.

We also need to talk about sharing intimate details. What happens behind closed doors is between you and your partner. It's nobody's business. Ever. Period. You don't share stories. You don't share photos. Period. Did I say period? Period. And about the photos: Before you send one, ask yourself whether you're OK with it being out in the world for everyone to see. Because intentionally or not, it *will* end up out there. Once it leaves your hands, you can't control it.

And when the relationship ends, even if badly, you never say anything about that person that isn't kind. This is not high school and you are a grown-up. Do your best to act like one. It's the right thing to do, and it will help avoid hurting their career or yours. People don't want to hear that nonsense, and it will change how they view you and your professionalism. Of course, I'm talking about typical relationships, not an abuse of power that leads to #MeToo moments, which are just the sorts of things that shouldn't be kept quiet.

As a practical matter, when dating in the workplace, make sure you keep it out of the workplace. Send your gooey messages of love on your own time, on your own devices; not on work time, not on work equipment. That sort of activity tends to end up not as private as you think, plus no one wants to see you two carrying on like gross high school love birds.

Even if you are trying to be careful, any assumption that your work email and messaging platforms are private is a bad assumption. A good assumption? That there could be a camera just about anywhere. Maybe not where you cleverly decided to meet, but coming and going, and that can be enough to trigger a problem.

And I wish I didn't have to say it, but when Johnny has this great idea about you and a desk, and after hours, remind him that he is a moron. You might very well get away with it, but you might not. Is the thrill worth your job?

Chapter 13: Mentors

If you are the smartest person in the room, you are in the wrong room. I read that somewhere years ago and it stuck.

I always sought the guidance and counsel of mentors, I just didn't know for a long time that's what I was doing. People who were smart, talented, and had more experience were magnets to me. It's amazing what you can learn from them. Then there came a point in my career where having mentors became an explicitly defined thing and they were chosen to help in my career and leadership development.

After years of growing with that help, I realized that it was getting harder to find people to mentor me and found myself wondering whether I was in the wrong room. While I still seek and still cherish when I do find those who can help, it dawned on me that the reason it was getting harder to find mentors was that it was time for me to give back to others. I was far enough along in my career that it was time to *be* the mentor; time to help others grow.

This was an important milestone – even though a little bittersweet in realizing what I was giving up. It's powerfully satisfying to be able to help someone else get stronger, but I do miss the days of being the one helped.

If you don't have a mentor, get one. Some companies have formal structures and processes for this. If yours does, use it. Seek it; don't wait for someone to come to you. Many companies won't have a formal process, so think about someone a level or two above you, someone you admire for how she operates, how she leads. And then just ask. The worst thing that will happen is she might say no, and that won't kill you, I promise.

As your career develops, this is a huge part of building your own network. It's not enough just to do your work well, you have to connect with the organization and your industry, and people have to actually see the work you do and the value you bring. You will also get access to a much broader range of knowledge and experience when you branch out like this.

A few tips that can help you get started:

- Don't pick someone just because you think they can help your career along. That's the wrong reason to seek a mentor and it won't go well. This shouldn't be a tactical move for your advancement, it's a strategic one for your long-term growth.
- Pick someone who is one or two levels above you and who has more years in the workforce than you do. It's usually best if they are not in your direct chain of command.
- Your mentor should be someone you admire for their knowledge and experience, and for their leadership.
- It should probably be someone in your organization, but it doesn't have to be. What's most important is that your mentor be someone who understands your professional world. In some ways, leading and managing are universal, but the culture, style, and structure of an organization matters. At the least, it should be someone in the same industry.

A few more tips after you get going:

- Assume it's on you to keep things moving. Your mentor probably has a lot of competing demands for her time, so taking on the task to reach out, to schedule, will likely be appreciated.
- Prepare for your time together. Think about what you want long term, and out of each session. Have questions.
- Don't use the time to get help with your work, or with promotions.
- Don't use the time to bitch about your boss or co-workers.
- Talk less, listen more. Really, that's good advice for life, but needs to be said here.

If you have been around long enough, and you have a couple of layers under you, then it's probably time for you to start giving back. There's a midpoint in your career where you can easily have a mentor and be a mentor too. They are not mutually exclusive. And I talk about having layers of management and staff over or under you, but sometimes these relationships can be more technical and less about managing or leading. Highly technical professions such as doctors, engineers, and sometimes lawyers often don't have deep organizational structures. Though the environment is different, the mentoring need is the same, and it can and should still be done.

You can also find mentors in peers who have been around longer than you, ones who might be willing to share their knowledge and experience.

And mentoring can come from outside of the work environment completely. For personal development, it could be a coach, a teacher, someone who works in your faith, sometimes even a friend.

When you get far enough along that it's harder to have traditional mentors, find peers you admire. There will be people in the same place you are, but who are on a bigger stage, or in a different environment. Establish a relationship and learn from them. Sometimes you'll both learn.

If you've never been a mentor before, start with this key guiding principle: This isn't time for you to just regale some poor trapped soul with stories about how amazing you are. This is time that's about the person you're helping. Your experiences and your stories will be relevant, but if you always focus on the person you are mentoring, seeking to understand what they know, and what they need, you will be far more effective as a mentor.

So go get a mentor, be a mentor, contribute to making a difference for others, not just you. And help make your organization better.

And remember, don't forget to thank them. They gave their time and experience just for you. Thank them when they do it, but make a point to go back later too, to let them know about something good that's happened in your life, and that they were one of the reasons you got there.

Chapter 14: The Magic of Teams

It's easy to make it all about you. In fact, we're wired to do that for lots of reasons that make sense for survival. And many of us grow up in homes that make us the focus, get us thinking that we're all the special magic little Ethans and Ashleys who are just going to be so darn amazing when we grow up to be president/influencer/astronaut/veterinarian/coder/entrepreneur.

Some of us experience team environments in high school or college, especially through sports. But so much of what we do is a solo effort, an effort that's all about ourselves. As we built our list of activities and service to get into college, then did it again to land that first job, it was always about us.

Then we end up in a real work environment for the first time, or we've moved into management, and discovering the magic of teams becomes key to so much success. What's the recipe? Listening, and actually using the work and ideas of others. Stepping back and letting others lead sometimes. Showing up, participating, and for the love of god, doing whatever work you are supposed to do by the time you are supposed to get it done.

That's all it takes.

If you're still reading after your brain told you this wasn't all about you (it lied, this still is all about you, just in a different way), let's talk about why teams are a wonderful thing in your life. They bring together more brains and more ideas than you have alone. This is good. Teams create more bandwidth than you have alone. This is also good. The old saying grandmas had about many hands making light work is, of course, true, because dammit, grandma was always right.

The "how" of being a good team member bears repeating: Show up. Do your part, and do it on time. Talk less, listen more. Actually use the ideas of others.

And maybe start accepting that it's possible someone else has an idea that's better than yours.

Recognize the value teamwork can bring. You can only do so much on your own; you only have so much time. Working with others can take some compromise, and it can take some extra effort up front. But in the end, you can tackle much bigger, much more complicated tasks and projects together. This is true not only of your time, but of your knowledge, your experience, and your problem-solving capabilities. Unless all your co-workers are actually idiots, (not just that you think they are), the team will bring more to the table in all of these areas than you can alone.

I know it can be frustrating. Especially when you're prepared and know what to do, and your partners are clueless and need you to hold their hand through the whole thing. You can be tempted to just give up and do it all yourself. But teamwork doesn't work like that.

There's a saying we have in my family when we're in the car: You can't go faster than the car in front of you. It's a gentle reminder to all of us about the things beyond our control.

For groups, you have to work at the pace they can handle even if it takes a lot of patience. It won't go well otherwise.

And have an appropriately positive attitude about your team and the work you're all doing. Why does this matter? Going into it with a lousy attitude, like it's a waste of time, will show not only in how the team reacts to you, but also in how you work in that environment.

If you're the type who thinks it's just easier to do it yourself, or that you already have all the answers, I challenge you to pretend you're wrong about both (because I probably can't get you to imagine that you are actually wrong about both) and try it out. If you can close your mouth and open your mind, you might be surprised.

A beautiful fringe benefit of teamwork is gaining the wisdom, experience and talents of others. Too many of us are reluctant to accept help. We don't want to appear weak or incapable, lacking knowledge or skill.

If you're young, you might not want to seem like you don't know your job. You might not feel like you've established yourself well enough yet. If you're older, you are expected to know what you're doing, right? So you can't appear like you don't. Asking for help can be even more difficult for underrepresented or marginalized groups, because of legacies of how their competencies are questioned.

We wrestle with these feelings, but if we accept them as normal, we can work to get past them. If you're the one offering the help, be mindful that people might be reluctant to accept for a variety of reasons and work to frame your offer in a way that's easier to accept. Stating the reason you're helping out loud can make a difference. Maybe you're helping because they are busy, or whatever the situation warrants, but say it. This extra step will help counter the feelings that feed their reluctance.

There are so many great reasons to make teamwork happen in your life. Everywhere in your life. And one more fringe benefit: Working with teams is a great way to develop your management and leadership skills. Getting people who don't work for you to work *with* you, to buy into your ideas and strategies, favors an encouraging, appreciative, and light-handed approach. If you can do that and have everyone not hate you, that's a good sign about your future as a leader.

Chapter 15: Taking the Back Seat

Taking the back seat is tough, especially in American culture in general, and in workplace culture in particular. We prize individuality; we focus on individual achievement. If you played a school sport, you probably heard the coach cliché that there's "no 'I' in team." They actually have to teach that and reinforce it. And in lots of sports, just like in the workplace, the stars want to shine, expect to shine, and expect everyone else to be supporting players to make them look good, to give them the stage to be large.

We are taught that we need to win, and to tell everyone about it. We are trained to curate our lives on social media in ways that show the world all the awesome things our awesome selves are doing. Even when we are telling the world about some great cause, most of the time we are also telling the world that we helped in that great cause, and aren't we just the best?

How can you even hope to take a back seat against all those odds? And some of you are asking, why would you want to?

Like some of the other ideas in this book, it's pretty easy to say, and it's harder to do. It takes work to build new ways of thinking and new habits.

Start here: Give credit; take the blame; praise others; talk less; listen more. Help others lead; help others shine. Encourage the quiet ones to speak up and the loud ones to hush. Do things that no one will know you did, things that you don't get any credit for.

I know, it's crazy, right? Why would you do that?

To be a better human. It's another thing that will make you the Decent Human Being I advocate for throughout the book. You will feel better. You will be happier. And whether you believe in karma or not, it will come back around.

Either do these things to be a better human, or at least to not appear like a bad one.

When you put yourself first, it shows. When you take the credit, pass the blame, and generally hog the stage, people notice. You will get a reputation for being *that* kind of person.

After getting past how much "me first" is driven into us growing up, one of the first challenges we face is that plenty of workplace cultures prize the selfish "star" behavior. This is especially so in high-pressure sales environments. Hell, the boss might be the worst offender.

So if you *have* to play the game, if you have to live in that kind of sandbox, at least you can always look for ways that do it with the least harm. You can still take the blame, share the credit, and help others shine, and all the other things too.

But you do have to be more careful that you get enough credit, that you don't take too much of the blame, that you sometimes shine, so you avoid being considered worthless and getting dumped. The point is, don't be an ass about it. And don't go overboard in taking the back seat either. There's a balance you have to find that works for you, and that works in your organization.

Chapter 16: Own It

In my first job after graduate school, in the first months of it even, I screwed up. We had a lot of new research data being collected, which was great for looking forward. But to go back more than a few years, we had to use old legacy data sets that were similar.

I did something stupid late one night and accidentally deleted them. All of them. This was before storage and backups were so cheap. It was before cloud storage even existed. Still, it was ridiculous that no one else had a copy, but there it was.

After a long night of cold sweat and visions of most certainly being fired, I walked into my boss's office and owned it. It was hard to do. I didn't have a track record yet to fall back on, one that might make it worth forgiving me. I survived this with my job *and* my integrity intact.

I have always believed that the combination of the fact that I tried all night to recover the data (and got half of it), that my boss was a Decent Human Being, that I was completely and sincerely sorry for what happened, and that I absolutely owned it all contributed to how this went. Had I done anything differently, it might easily have gone another way.

Maybe you've had something happen that made you look terrible, or cost your organization time, money, or reputation. I hope not. It sucks.

It's almost a reflex. When blame, or even just criticism, comes our way, we turn into a child who doesn't want to disappoint, to fail, to feel bad. So we react – maybe without even thinking – to push the blame somewhere else, to say "it wasn't my fault."

Add in a layer in places such as the corporate world where your mistakes can cost reputation, money, and legal trouble, and this can encourage another shortcut: to say nothing, accept no blame, no responsibility.

These are real challenges that fall into the easy-to-say, hard-to-do category I mention all the time in this book.

Start here though: Can you picture a time when someone got called out, got questioned, and she said something like "Yep, that was me. Crap. Sorry. I will implement some changes to prevent it from happening again, and would appreciate it if we can talk about how to fix it this time."? It's powerful, direct, and sadly not common enough. She owned it. Like a grown-up, not a child.

Being a grown-up is key here, as it is in lots of places throughout this book. Being a Decent Human Being and not being silent or blaming others is important too. Don't be a weasel.

Often, how you handle it – or don't – can be more damaging than the mistake itself. A prime example: People are late all the time. It can range from a few minutes to an absurd amount of time. And the impact of being late can range from a minor annoyance to causing real problems. This can hurt your reputation, your relationships, your career. What can you do? Damage control. Minimize the impact. Make a phone call. Give someone a heads up. Make a new plan if needed. Most of the time this will make all the difference. And it shows respect for others, even if you meant no disrespect by being late. Ignoring it screams a lack of it.

If you want yet another reason besides being a grown-up: It's efficient with your time and everyone else's. Own it. Get in front of it for damage control, and don't waste everyone's time with long and winding excuses and thin stories that no one believes. You know you've heard some spokesperson avoid responsibility, avoid blame, deny the reality. You know it was obviously nonsense, and you lost some respect for that person and that organization that day. Don't do that. Don't be that.

There are plenty of ways to accept responsibility without trashing yourself or the company. You don't want to make it worse by damaging the trust and confidence people have in your organization. And you also don't want to damage how they feel either. When people get a negative impression, it tends to reinforce – and be reinforced by – the dark clouds in the office (See Chapter 33, Are You a Dark Cloud?). And that negative impression will spiral; it will spread.

So how do you accept responsibility without wreaking havoc? This might sound a little contradictory, but be positive about it. Don't be gloomy. Don't trash those involved or the company. Be measured, polite, accurate, and open. Don't get defensive and try to explain the world's history, or yours, that led to that moment.

One of the best ways to help you accept responsibility well is to be brief. Most of us have a strong tendency to defend ourselves (or our organization), so disciplining yourself to be brief can help you stay focused and avoid blaming others or trying to fudge what really happened to make it look like it's not bad. If you blame others or minimize the issue, people will see right through it and you will lose.

So step up, be a grown-up, and own it. It's like a workout. You might hurt a bit, but you will get stronger. You'll feel better. Your confidence will grow and your ability to lead will develop broader shoulders.

PART II: It's All About You

You're all special. No one is special.

You're all unique. You're all the same.

You are amazing, confident, and strong. You are a nervous wreck of insecurity and doubt.

Everyone else is incredible and has their shit together. You're a mess.

All of their lives are amazing, just look at their stories. It's all curated nonsense; a real-life reality show.

Talk about mixed messages. Talk about confusing and contradictory. Sometimes it feels like there are only two kinds of people: those who, through simple blissful ignorance (or spectacular ego), seem to be Doing Just Fine, and everyone else who is a basket of broken things. The world hurts. The world is full of wonder and joy. Knowledge is pain. Knowledge is inner peace, wisdom, and understanding. They muddle through. Good days and bad. Happiness always tempered.

It's probably a spectrum, a bell curve, like so many other things. Spectacular highs, crushing lows. A whole bunch in between. Mixed emotions, ups and downs. This is Life. But it is *your* life.

In the upcoming chapter "Be You, Just Less," I make the case for keeping the parts of you that overwhelm others in check. But let me flip this around here and argue that you need to be *you*, all of you. Sometimes *more* of you. Not someone else, not someone's idea of who you are, not your idea of what someone else's idea of you is.

Personal growth is about learning. It's about evolving and improving. But a big part is about learning to like who you are, to be OK in your own skin, to like what you like and not be embarrassed about it.

Because it's all about you. And in many ways, it really should be. It's your life. No one will live it for you (though some will certainly try to direct the movie that is your life). Even all the things you do to help others are still part of your life, of your experience.

These next chapters are here to guide you toward a better you, a stronger you, and maybe help sand off some rough edges so that polished surface can shine more brightly.

Chapter 17: Be You, Just Less

One of my corporate colleagues, when confronted by one of my all-too-common rants about something or other, would stop me, look me in the eyes, and say calmly and quietly "Be you, just less." It was powerful advice and it stuck with me. It gets at something so important throughout this book: The intent is not to change you into someone else, something you're not, it is to help you be a better version of you, of who you already are.

What is that one thing about you that's just too much? Hopefully you know the answer to this. If you don't think inwardly all that much, this is a good place to start. If you think the answer is "Nothing, I'm amazing," then maybe you spend too much time looking in the mirror and not enough time looking at yourself through other people's eyes.

If you know, great, and if you don't, figure it out. It won't be hard, you just have to ask people who know you well, and you have to ask in a way that they will feel comfortable telling you. Saying "Am I annoying?" will not likely get you an honest answer, except from a rare friend, or maybe your mom. Saying, for example, "Do you think other people might find me annoying?" might work better. Don't try to force a close friend, family member, or co-worker to tell you something lousy about yourself. Frame it about how others might perceive you.

Maybe you're loud, aggressive, or crude. Maybe you think you're super funny but are actually just snarky and mean. Maybe you care deeply about, oh, about almost anything, and you drown everyone in it, not even considering whether they care as much as you do about whatever esoterica floats your boat.

I mean, it's delightful that you know every detail about some video game series, or the evolution of passenger jets, or the intricate workings of a mechanical clock. But almost no one else cares, and they really don't want to hear much about it. Same holds true for those of you who know something about almost everything. No one cares.

There are two big worst-offender categories that so many of us fall into when it comes to going on and on: our hobbies and our workouts. I know you are excited about your hobby and proud of the workout you did, but again, no one cares.

No one wants to hear about how you crushed that last set and how sore your quads are from that massive workout. And no one wants to hear about the 14 new bottles in your hipster artisanal craft beer collection. I could go on for 10 minutes about the run I did this morning. Who would want to hear that? No one.

There's a strategy to help with this that I love: Wait until you are asked. If the many uses for chickpeas comes up, by all means, offer up your encyclopedic knowledge. But if no one asks, just let it simmer.

If you do share your experiences or talk about your collections, make it brief and be sure it's part of the conversation and not the whole thing.

For another group, numbing people's brains with your fascination about the various types of honey isn't the problem. For this next group, it's oversharing, it's Too Much Information. You know something happens a lot when there's commonly used shorthand: TMI.

There are two big buckets of this. The first is just plain oversharing. Too much detail on a topic that just doesn't need it. Saying you're late because you had a flat tire or your alarm didn't go off is enough. Telling the 15-minute version of why you had a flat tire that involves complex relationship dynamics and LOTS of background detail is just soul-deadening to the people around you.

The second type is the true TMI. Like how the cauliflower rice you eat all the time makes you a giant fart bag. No one wants to hear that (or the farting, if that's not obvious). And the date you went on last night? Seriously, keep the details to yourself, for a variety of reasons that are spelled out all over this book.

On top of the general guidance here to say less, share less, the best way to guide yourself is to pay attention to context, to your audience, and to the time and place. What might be perfectly appropriate conversation over drinks with friends, might be terribly off in a work meeting. Using your judgment, hell, gaining some judgment, will do you great service. It requires you to look at yourself to see what needs restraint, some emotional intelligence (see Chapter 31, Who ARE You?), and taking the time to Read the Room (see Chapter 26).

A key theme to this book is to be you, just less, and at the same time, to be you, just more. This might sound contradictory, but they both push you to be a better you, just in different directions.

One way is to nourish, amplify and reinforce all the good things about you. The other way is to dial back the volume of You when it's too loud, and polish the rough spots that will let you shine.

Spending this chapter talking about being less makes it important to highlight the value of being *more* of you too. It comes up more than once in this book, but it's important that you are still you. If you are holding back too much of you, you will be flat, uninteresting, and invisible. And you'll blame me. Neither of us wants that. We still want the genuine you. The right you in the right context. In other words...

Be you, just less.

Chapter 18: Habit Forming

Just about everyone has tried to change something; to start or end a behavior. And most of the time, they failed. There are reasons for this, and if you know them up front, you can vastly increase your chances of success by making some small adjustments.

The first adjustment is to recognize when the change you want to make is unreasonable, when it doesn't fit you, or when the expectation you set is too high. You decide you want to learn a new language, or to play the violin. These are reasonable. But if you don't even know English well or set too short a timeline for the task, learning another language is too much to ask. You will get frustrated and quit. It's the same with the violin example. To learn an instrument takes time, effort, and lots of repetitive practice.

If words such as "time," "effort," and "practice" aren't part of your normal world, then this effort won't go well for you. Step one is to ask yourself whether the desired change is really you, and whether you can – or truly want to – put in the time and effort to make it happen. Be real with yourself here; no wishful thinking allowed.

The second adjustment is to give yourself a reasonable timeline. Too often, we try to make a change the same way you turn on a light. For nearly everyone, it takes more than flipping a switch. Sure, I know people who, through sheer force of stubborn will, have made big changes. But they are weirdos. Exceptions.

The rest of us have much more success making changes in our lives when we start slow and build gradually. Let's say you want to eat better and like a New Year's resolution, you swear off all the sugary, fatty, carb-y, and salty things that fill the world with deliciousness. Just like that, you've made the change. But it's abrupt, and you're miserable. For all but the most determined of us, this effort is doomed.

New runners all too often head out the door, determined to run a few miles. It's miserable, and after a few days, the experience of doing something unpleasant, and being sore as your reward, is enough to get most people to drop it.

I always tell running clients that they should be able to carry on an easy conversation during the run, even if that means walking some. They need to take it slow. Don't go out and try to kill it. You'll make it a quarter of a mile before you feel like lying down right there in the street. This is the same with most habits you want to start or end. Start small. Start slow. Build.

The third adjustment is about your real priorities. I read this phrase once and it really stuck: "Your actions are your priorities." This distills into a few words the idea that if you aren't doing something you want to do, then it probably wasn't as important as something else you are doing. You might want to be more active and lose some weight, but if you decide that munching on delicious snacks and sitting on the couch in front of a screen is better, well, that's probably what you will keep doing. The same holds true for being too busy to start working out, or learning a new skill, or painting that room. You're not too busy, it's just that whatever you're doing is more important, regardless of what you say about the thing you want to do.

To build a new habit or end an old one: Be reasonable. Be realistic. Start small and build up slowly. And make sure what you think you want is really what you want. [2]

---

[2] James Clear wrote a book on habits that I think is fantastic. The approach he articulates so well involves making the new habit obvious, easy, attractive, and satisfying. Definitely worth a read.

Chapter 19: Hard Things & Scary Things

For some of us, there is excitement, even joy, about trying new things, about going to new places. I know a few people who will go to movies and restaurants alone. That sounds like nothing, but really, not many people would be OK doing that. That's more in the bucket of Awkward or Uncomfortable Things than it is in the bucket of Hard Things and Scary Things. But it's all part of the same idea: For most of us, we avoid lots of things in life – sometimes consciously, often not.

Why? The awkward and uncomfortable things are often anything we do that's outside "normal" or "expected." We don't want to stand out. Even if we really would like to be noticed or the center of attention, a bigger part of us doesn't want to stand out.

The difference is often guided by what we think "looks" good or bad to others. You might want to be noticed for how good you look or how well you do something, but not so much for anything you view as negative or that stands out *too* much. Maybe you feel like eating alone makes you look like a friendless loser instead of someone who happened to be alone and was hungry.

This fear keeps us from going alone to eat, or to a movie, or a concert. It keeps us from wearing that outfit we have that's bold and out-of-the-box. It keeps us from really expressing our own preferences, our own desires, and we just go along with the crowd and get what we get. It keeps us from trying new things.

The antidote to this? You can find it in a cliché about women over 40. At some point lots of women get comfortable in their skin. They stop worrying about what they look or sound like to others. They start focusing on themselves and their happiness. They say and do what they want. The takeaway for everyone at all ages is to think about the why: Why are you avoiding doing the thing? Be honest. If it has anything to do with what others will think or say, then practice, with baby steps, not letting that get in your way.

We avoid the hard things because they are hard and the scary things because they are scary. But why? Fear of failure mostly, in our own eyes and in the eyes of others. We don't want others to see us as less than we think we are, and we darn sure don't need evidence to lower that internal measure of our awesomeness. Proof is inconvenient.

We avoid things to escape the possibility of embarrassment or ridicule, especially in public. The classic avoidance is public speaking. I think these are the reasons so many people don't want to do it.

Other reasons we run from hard things and scary things? Actual injury, or even death. Injury to our professional standing. Risk of job loss, financial loss, broken friendships and relationships. Risk of death. These are bad, so we use them as excuses to do nothing.

What else can you do to get more comfortable with hard things and scary things? Find some tools, some guides, that work for you. One of my favorites is to think about the Cost of Being Wrong. And "cost" here means anything, not just money. You can use this to set your risk tolerance for anything. The lower the cost of being wrong, or of failing, the easier it is to do it anyway. The things with a high cost need more careful consideration, more planning, to balance the benefit against the cost of failure. This strategy can let you set your own personal boundaries for new things.

Another tool: Don't borrow tomorrow's problems. We talked about this earlier, and I know it sounds like something a grandma would say, but it's powerful when you apply it regularly. It's useful, calming, and can bring clarity and order to your thinking.

It doesn't mean that you shouldn't worry about anything, or that you shouldn't plan for anything. It means only worry about the stuff that matters now, and don't worry about the stuff that hasn't happened yet. You can get bogged down so quickly and become unable to make a move.

Let's say you were trying to figure out where you were going to college, and then your brain went off on some wild journey about what clothes you might need. Well, until you know the culture and the climate, the clothes decisions just don't matter. Or maybe you were planning where you were going to live after you graduated. Getting wired up about what furniture you need in your new place is just not important until you figure out where you're going and then where you will live. Furniture is a few steps down the list, and you can just let it go until it's relevant.

If you try to figure out everything, for every step of the way, in each scenario that could happen depending on all the things that happened before, your brain will overload, and you'll find yourself curled up in a ball under a desk. It *is* good to have *general* ideas about the things you would do later depending on what happens first, because it can actually help make the decisions you face now easier. General Ideas. Not every last detail of every last option.

Next, try to plan your failures. I know that might seem dark, but hear me out. My daughter was prepping for an important language exam that would allow her to study overseas. She was carrying all sorts of anxiety about failing the exam, because it would mean she couldn't start classes when she planned. Definitely a big deal for her.

So I asked: "What happens if you fail?" I mean, besides how much it would suck. The answer was she would have to see whether there was time to take the next exam and get the results before the semester enrollment deadline. Tight, but possible, it seemed. OK, great. What happens if the deadline is too tight, or you *do* get to take it again, but you fail again? Super sucks still, I know. But the answer was that she'd have to wait an entire semester to get started while she tried the prep and the exam again.

My point in all of this, and yes, I do have one, is that it can take a lot of stress off the thing weighing on you if you've already figured out what you'd do next (and next, and next) if it goes poorly. Having that added perspective, almost a worst-case-scenario view, can make the decisions you need to make first that much easier to make. And it also makes it easier not to borrow tomorrow's problems if you more or less know what you'd do if the first one or two things go wrong.

Another one of the tools I use is to always try to say yes. Not to things I don't want to do for good reasons. I am a grown-ass man and happy to say no. (It's liberating, by the way, if you haven't done much of the saying no). I say yes to new things that sound interesting or scary or hard. When asked to speak in public, I say yes. When asked to do something like scuba dive or jump out of an airplane, I say yes. When asked to go somewhere new or try some new food, I say yes. It's always an experience, even if it's one I don't want to repeat. This strategy is a big help because the fear of doing hard or scary things gives the brain an incentive to reject them (because they are hard or scary). Being intentional in your thinking process will help you avoid saying no for the wrong reasons.

Yet another tool: Look for a way to reframe. I was nominated for an award recently, and as part of the process, the organization wanted me to explain in detail and in writing why I am so awesome and deserving. This checks a lot of boxes: Awkward and uncomfortable to brag about yourself. Fear of failure or embarrassment when I lose out to another finalist in front of everyone. I was totally going to skip it, to ignore the nomination. Then I thought: Well, at least the judges will see all that I've done. So maybe those few people will know I've tried to do good stuff for others. And you know what? That reframe made it enough. So I did the thing.

Overcoming discomfort and fear equates with growth. It equates to our own evolution. It allows us to experience new things; to learn new things we like and those we don't care to repeat. It allows us to find more things and more people who fit us better. It allows us to live life better. And facing your fears makes it a little easier to do the next time.

Ever since my kids were little, we've had Rule No. 1 in our house. If you asked them what Rule No.1 is, they'd roll their eyes a little, and say in unison: "Don't Die."

What does it mean? Well, obviously, it literally means don't die. This is a big one. And it's not just some safety lecture or always being overly cautious.

We instilled this in them because it's so important to take care of yourself. They'd be headed into the world soon enough, and would be responsible for themselves. They'd see new things and try new things. And they'd be in weird situations sometimes.

So part of this – for those who are parents – is how important our kids are to us.

But it's really about something much different. When it comes to living, to trying things that are hard or scary, it's about taking the room to learn and grow – and to help remind you what the outer boundary should be. That what you should be doing is pretty much anything you want. Up to that dying point.

It's about being able to live your life however you want. It's about not being held back by fear – of failure, of ridicule, of anything really. It's about not being held back by too much caution or others' expectations or conventions.

And all it requires is getting comfortable with a little risk, tempered with just a smidgen of good judgment and thoughtfulness. That's it.

So live, have fun, learn and grow. Try new things. Try hard things and scary things. And let this be your outer boundary: Don't die.

Chapter 20: Time

There is an old saying that youth is wasted on the young. Time is what drives this sentiment. It seems endless and abundant when you're young. (Excepting those who by choice or circumstance juggle a lot in high school or college.) Even with jobs, or taking care of siblings, or a life devoted to excellence in sports or music, whatever it may be, most of us found lots of time to play. Or to do nothing.

Then we enter the workforce and a ton of time starts getting taken up, time that is – or at least feels – outside of our control. Then we partner up. And more of our time (hopefully, willingly and gladly), becomes not just about ourselves. Then we have kids, and 20 years later, we might be able to take a breath.

We're 40 or 50 now. The time feels fast. The train we're on is careening down a mountain and maybe we feel like we can see the station way off in the distance and there's nothing we can do to stop it or even slow it down...

Time is the single-most precious thing we have. Whether you're 25 or 55, the two most important things we can do with it are to live well and to live fully. This is true no matter what your focus becomes, whatever the mix of family, career, and community drives you, living fully and living well will help you make the most of the time you have.

One of the idle intellectual musings I have is this: What do you think a 60-year-old billionaire would pay to be 30 again? My bet is that it would be a staggering amount.

What can you do?

Think about how you use your time. Mindlessly scrolling on your phone, sitting in front of streaming video, or playing games for hours on end can be fun – and a way to unwind. But if it becomes your default activity, a routine habit, then it would be good to ask yourself whether there's something that's more valuable to you that you could be doing. It's like how drinking a bit of wine regularly can be pleasant, maybe even healthy. But slamming two bottles every night, we all know, is not going to end well.

Let's focus on the workplace first though. Work will take a huge chunk of time from most of us.

The flow at work is faster, the pace is faster, since we moved into the world of instant communication. The past 10, maybe 20 years, are fundamentally different. Many of you in the workforce today never experienced the "before time" when things were slower and required snail mail to communicate, printed newspapers to see what was going on, and waiting a week to see the next episode of a show, a year for the next season.

This pace of *right now* is all you know. The key here is to become adept at managing it. And if you have been around long enough to remember the before time, the key is also not wishing today's time was something else. If this instant way is all you've experienced of time, then your challenge is to control it (for you) and not be swept up in its flow.

For many professionals, the work is never done; only you can control your schedule. It is rare that anyone will do this for you. There is another old saying that goes something like: No one ever says on their deathbed that they wished they had worked more.

There are times when we need to work and forsake just about everything else: Times of crisis, times of transition, special projects, and so on. But this time where we live in a state of triage needs to have an end date. If it's how you live every day, you will miss out on living, and it will wear you out. Hard.

There are times we make choices to be crazy busy, such as working full time while getting a degree, or choosing a career that requires a ton of work and time to get going, like becoming a doctor, or starting your own business. But these choices have gains, they have outcomes you want.

It's critical that you ask yourself: "What am I getting from these 60-100 hour weeks?" If the answer is essentially, "I have a job," it's time to rethink it. Dumping all your time into work needs to have an outcome that is worth it to you, and burning the candle at both ends (a saying that makes sense, but is weird when you think about it) can't go on forever.

People say how incredibly busy they are. We hear it all the time. In my coaching work, or when I am facilitating strategic planning sessions, I tell them "Busy" is not a competition. "Busy" is not a badge of honor. It is failure. It means you're not managing your time and your priorities. Most everything we do is a choice. It often doesn't feel that way for sure, but they are.

A few tips: First, get rid of low-value work, tasks, and habits. I always changed the oil in my cars, mostly because I liked the work. At some point though, having someone else do it became easy (no appointment, just pop in and pop out at an oil-change place), and it became cheap. It cost less than the value of my time, so I punted that task. I use this model all the time. Does the thing cost me less to have someone else do it than the value of my time?

Now sometimes this choice is also guided by how much we can spend. Let's say you can paint that room in your home in a day for $50 of materials or you can pay someone $250 to do it. But if you don't have $250 to spend, that has to be factored in the calculation too.

The other typical exceptions are things you like to do even if they aren't cost-effective. My wife likes to mow the lawn because it's therapeutic in a way. It's sort of mindless and the opposite of her daily work. It's definitely not worth her time to do it, but it makes her happy. Happy has value.

Here's another tip: Practice staying on your current focus; on whatever's important to you right now. You may be dealing with a constant barrage of messages, texts, or emails. But have you been trained, or even trained yourself unknowingly, to respond instantly to every new thing? Like we talked about in Chapter 1, Put Your Phone Down, shifting your attention to every new thing is hurtful, insulting, or at least annoying, to whomever you are with, and rapid task-switching has a cost to you in quality and speed.

One more tip: Aside from whatever is buzzing or dinging right now, I'm always tempted to dive into what's easiest or most interesting on my list. But I have developed a habit of starting with what's most important every day. And when that's done, or moved ahead far enough, I start knocking out the rest. It's amazing how liberating it is to have a big thing done every morning and the rest of the day feels more peaceful even though I am still doing a bunch of other things.

When I was writing this book, the first thing I did most days was work on a chapter. That was the best way for me to make sure I actually got this done. Then I could catch up on all the other things I needed to do and what everyone else needed from me.

And of the things outside of work that people want you to do, ask yourself this question: Do I *want* to do it? This is a great tool to evaluate how you spend your time.

When someone asks whether you want to go to a show, or an exhibit, or a get-together or a family thing, or a fundraiser, or whatever: If you peel away friendships, family, guilt, obligations, and habit, ask yourself whether you *want* to do it. If you say to yourself, "You know, that [charity fundraiser gala, or softball tournament or you-fill-in-the-blank thing] sounds like fun, and I want to go," then you should. If the answer is "No," then you can more rationally weigh the importance of the other things: things such as family peace, of giving of yourself, whatever the case may be, to see whether that's enough to outweigh the "no" answer.

In the end, time is all we have. Cherish it. Value it. Cherish the things you do, and the people close to you.

And for the record, naps are a valuable use of time.

Chapter 21: How Do You Recharge?

One of the best explanations I've seen for whether you are an introvert or an extrovert is to look at how you recharge. When her human battery runs down, one of my daughters heads out the door. She recharges by doing things, going places, engaging with others. The other daughter is the opposite. She heads to her room, settles deep into her secure nest, and spends time alone. She could be reading a book, scrolling through Tumblr blogs, writing, or watching a show. But what tops off her human battery is peace, quiet, security, and most importantly, no crowds.

I like this way of looking at it because introverts *can* enjoy themselves out in the world, even in social situations and crowds. It's just that at some point, they've had enough and want to get away from it all.

And extroverts can enjoy quiet time alone, or with just one or two others. But at some point, they get antsy and feel a magnetic pull toward the energy of the world at large.

What's important in all this is to figure out which you are and do it that way. Learn to monitor your own battery. Even if that means taking a different path than your group sometimes. You do you.

And we need to emphasize the "do it" part. Because even if you know how to manage You, if you're not doing it, you will wear out.

Take a look at what you do to take care of you. We seem to just pick up bits and pieces about self-care as we move out into the world. It's not taught. It's not explicit. It might even seem elitist, pampering, soft, or selfish.

But you have needs, things that will help you be happy and healthy. And it's a place to park the judgment of others too. I always thought getting a massage was for well-off, spoiled people with time on their hands. It was a little bit of my own bias, my own judginess shining through. But once, after a really long and grueling running race, I had to get straight onto a long flight to meet my family for vacation time halfway across the country. My cooped-up, post-race legs were trashed. So my wife marched me right to a spa and sent me in there for a massage. This was self-care for her via not having to put up with me being broken and whiny. Anyway, this was no pampering. Some hulk of a dude laid into my legs and worked them over hard. There were definitely tears at one point. But it worked. It was amazing. I started incorporating massages into my training cycles at key points.

Some people get their nails done, go to a yoga class, or sit in a sauna. Some people take a walk in the woods, take a nap, or go out for a nice meal. Some people shoot hoops, go for a run, or ride a bike. Doesn't matter what. What matters is that you think about the things that help you recharge, the things that bring you a little rest, a little peace, a little happiness. And then make sure you find the time to do them.

For some of us, that means blocking out time on the calendar and sticking to it. Because it is almost always the easiest thing to blow off to use the time or the money for something else. So taking care of yourself, especially for those who tend to put others first, can be a challenge. But even if you are one to take care of others first, if you can't function well yourself, how can you take care of others?

As part of the workday, I incorporate what I call Health and Safety Breaks, or HSBs. Since I have my own business and set my own schedule, my tendency is to just keep working. I always have a list of physical stuff to do, and so I get up from my desk every hour or two and do something. I fix, install, build, or clean something. I love tools and this stuff makes me happy. Figure out the kinds of short interludes you can take during the time you work. Do something satisfying that gets you up from your desk. Take a quick walk. Do *something*.

And finally, you've all probably heard about work/life balance. I like to think more in terms of life balance. Many of us don't have rigid and defined work schedules. Work happens all the time. Or at least it can and will if we let it. So thinking about ourselves, and our own health and happiness overall is helpful. And looking at everything at work and everything outside of work as a zero-sum game where if one side "wins" the other side "loses" is less helpful. Striving to make the balance better in your life is healthier, and more achievable, and will cause less tension between your work world and the rest of your life.

How do *you* recharge?

Chapter 22: Career Choices

The choice you made for a career – whether that happened in college, or high school, or even earlier – might have sounded cool, interesting, or important. Or maybe it was something that runs in the family so you naturally gravitated toward it, consciously or not. Maybe there was an expectation in the family that you'd follow in their footsteps or join a family business. Maybe you just sort of stumbled into a career without really much thought at all. Hell, maybe you don't yet know what you want to do with your life.

If you are already working in this career though, it's good to stop to ask: Am I on the right path? If you are, that's great. If you're not, you *can* make a change. Depending on what you've invested in time, money, and effort, it might be difficult, but it can be done. My dorm neighbor in college was studying engineering, but what he really wanted was to be a chef. How often do you think people just stuff away that dream, that urge, and keep plugging along on the current path?

If you are feeling flat, or full-on miserable, in your work, then you might be in the wrong role, the wrong company, or even the wrong profession. I know people who were really satisfied *doing* their jobs, but once they moved up to *managing* the work, they weren't getting that satisfaction anymore. Some people find much more meaning in hands-on doing, than in managing or leading. It's OK to prefer any of these. It's your life and this is all about you.

It's important to look at who you are to make sure what you're doing is a good fit for your personality, for your style. Where you land on the introverted/extroverted spectrum matters a lot, as does how smart you are, and your level of social skill. Take a look at Chapter 31, Who ARE You?, and Chapter 21, How Do You Recharge?

Then, do a little self-check to see whether you find meaning in what you're doing. You might hear a lot about being happy or loving what you do, but I think more along the lines of finding meaning. It is work after all, so it might not be a source of happiness. But finding value in what you do, finding the work meaningful, is a key driver of whether you're in the right place.

Also ask yourself whether what you're doing is what you expected. A new lawyer might have thought she was going to help the helpless and is now spending 80 hours a week reviewing contracts. Sometimes our ideas about a career end up being a lot less like the things we learned from books and movies. If this is the case for you, then maybe changing focus a little is all you need. That lawyer might take a pay cut and trade the salary for public-defender or interest-group work, for example. So while she's on the right general path, a different road might be better.

But if you have a general sense the work is not you at all, then it's time for a few more questions. The profession might be what you thought it was, but it turns out it's not really a good fit for you. Or it might be completely different than what you thought, and again, not a good fit.

Start with what motivates you. It could be money, status, power, contribution to society, security, helping others, or just a means to an end, a paycheck so you can live your life.

Simplify the questions: do you want a job or a career? I look at a job as something you do for a steady paycheck so you can take the money you earn and live your life. Maybe nothing in the work world seems all that interesting to you, but the stuff you do outside of work really does. If this is you, then your calculation needs to balance how much you make, how much you need to work to earn it, how secure the job is, whether you sit at a desk, or are out in the world, and whether you have to travel. You are the one who gets to decide the weight of the variables like these.

And if you want money – not a paycheck, but money – lots of it, then your calculation changes. It's more along the lines of what careers maximize earnings in the shortest time, factoring in the amount of training and education required to get there. Those are the slides on the mixing board you need to balance.

If you want to help others, then see what pulls at your heartstrings the hardest, and prepare yourself emotionally and practically to accept a more modest lifestyle because of the lower salaries that come with so many of those careers.

I listed money, power, and status as separate items, but in some ways, they are all the same thing. If you have one of them, you probably have the others. In many roles, money, status, and power go hand in hand. What doesn't come automatically is making a contribution to society. In professions that are all about making money, if you want to have that kind of societal impact too, you have to choose to spend it in ways to make that contribution.

Then again, some professions are all about impact and contribution. People give their time and talents, much like so many do at a local nonprofit or for a cause, but they focus and strive, and they grow to a level where they can make a difference at a larger scale. Sometimes a global scale.

One thing that is woven into all of these is the question of what you are capable of doing. It doesn't matter what you *want* to do if it's not really in your wheelhouse to do it. And it also doesn't matter what you want to do if no one wants to pay you to do it.

Evaluate the answers, *your* answers, to these: What can I do better than others? What will the world pay me to do? What will I find meaning in doing? And you can swap out "meaning" for: What problems do I want to solve, or How do I want to be known?

Once you find the intersection of those answers, you should have a good idea of whether you're in the right place, and if not, where you should go.

Chapter 23: Undisciplined Thing

Meet Dave. He's smart, capable, and definitely a Decent Human Being. But Dave can be a mess. He's great at planning when it comes to work projects, but when it comes to his own life, not so much. Dave likes to wing it. He has a fundamental belief that it'll all work out. And you know what? It usually does. This reinforces Dave's outlook on life.

When he travels, he packs at the last minute. So what if he forgets a toothbrush – he can just buy one when he gets there. Of course, Dave always leaves for the airport with the amount of time it *should* take to get there. If there's some traffic, whatever. It'll be fine. He always makes it before they close the door on the plane.

This is all fine. Dave can be Dave, and the rest of us can sit back and smile as we watch these things unfold. But there are two places it matters: The first is when the cost of this Dave-ness is high enough to matter to him. The second is when it impacts others.

Dave forgets his wallet sometimes. No Big Deal, he says, he knows where it is. And he's never been pulled over when he doesn't have it. And he can pay for stuff with his phone. NBD (and he says NBD a *lot*). But if Dave forgets his wallet going to the airport, they will not let him on the plane, and he doesn't have time to go get it. He misses the flight. This affects Dave's life. This is bad.

Dave rarely puts anything on his calendar. Work stuff sometimes, sure. Meetings mostly. Sometimes he's smart enough to put a deadline on there too. But outside of work? Nothing. He just remembers stuff. It all works out. Maybe that present to his mom for her birthday gets there a day late. NBD.

She understands. Maybe he's late for something because he didn't remember until the last minute. NBD, he got there. He was only a little late. Although sometimes if it's a morning thing, a lunchtime thing or a thing right after work, he just misses it entirely. He was busy, right? In the zone. These affect other people's lives. This is also bad.

In the workplace, usually there are enough not-Daves on the team to keep things from becoming a disaster. But you can't count on that. Plus, Daves put more work on everyone else, while irritating them in the process.

And while we're here, meet Jen. She's Dave's boss. They are both cut from the same cloth. While he is a leaf happily floating downstream, she is a whirlwind of chaos. When combined, it's spectacular to watch and painful to be a part of.

Jen recently moved to another city a few hundred miles away. And then she needed to jump on a plane for a meeting, but she was out of her blood pressure meds, which she probably needed because of Dave. NBD, right? Just call the pharmacy and they will have it refilled today, and she doesn't leave until the morning. Easy. But wait, the prescription has no refills. NBD, right? Just call the doctor's office and get her to update it. But wait, she missed her last appointment and hasn't had a check-up in a year, so doc can't refill it until she looks at her. And guess where doc is? Hundreds of miles away in the city she left behind.

What's the big takeaway here? Every problem here was caused by Jen's basic lack of planning and attention to detail. You wouldn't know that from listening to her rage against the universe for screwing her over so much. But we know.

There's an old saying that would be printed and stuck up on someone's office wall or cubicle as a warning: Poor Planning on Your Part Does Not Constitute an Emergency on Mine. Now it's a T-shirt and meme too. This is not a new problem; it's a classic. And all of this gets at the biggest point here (and I'm going to start a new line because this needs to stand out all by itself):

Everything that goes wrong in your life is your fault.

OK, *most* of what goes wrong is your fault, but I liked the way it sounded. Sometimes that fender bender was because of someone else, not because you were in a hurry or not really paying attention. And sometimes crappy things just happen. They do. We all know this. But *most* of it is on us.

If you're a Dave or a Jen, what can you do? What should you do?

The first goal here is to not make your life any harder than it needs to be. The second goal is to not make everyone else's lives any harder than they need to be.

What does this mean? It's about learning to manage You. Don't just try harder. That's nearly always the wrong answer. You have to do something *differently.* And don't try to be something you are not. It's a key concept in this book: Keeping you who you are. Because, of course, you are special and wonderful. And because it's a lot easier to edit your life than it is to rewrite it completely.

I talk elsewhere in the book about the Cost of Being Wrong. It's a great tool to evaluate risk. Let's birth its twin: The Cost of Failure. Decide which things you care enough about to do something about. And then do just enough to avoid consequences you don't want. If you use the Cost of Failure as your guide, as a quick gut-check, you can avoid most of them. You can keep packing at the last minute and keep forgetting your toothbrush, but not your wallet. So Dave starts putting out on the counter near his front door anything he really can't afford to leave behind. He starts using his calendar to remind him to do stuff. That's it. And he still gets to be Dave, who is just so chill.

What about Jen? She's a wreck. Just leave her be.

And really, when I talk about learning to manage You, it's about planning and preparing, it's about thinking ahead. We all are on a continuum somewhere of how much we do this. The Cost of Failure model is a way to help you move along that continuum just enough to be OK. See Chapter 18, Habit Forming, for a little guidance on how to do it.

This chapter title, "Undisciplined Thing," comes from my time at Marine Corps boot camp. Picture a bunch of high school graduates, mostly clueless. And picture these tough-as-nails drill instructors who are trying to turn us into functioning humans and then level us up into functioning Marines. No small task. They yelled. A lot. All. The. Time.

"Undisciplined Thing" was what my instructors called us every time we did something stupid, something sloppy, something that reeked of failure. Imagine it in an angry, disappointed, biting growl. *Buncha undisciplined things.*

What if you have a Dave or a Jen in your life? What can you do? Be kind to them. Be patient. They are probably DHBs. Help them if you can, as a peer, as a mentor. But most of all, protect yourself. Have a backup plan in case they fail you. Use gentle reminders to help them do the thing you need them to do.

And if you are Dave's opposite, the one who plans *everything, always,* at home, at work, in relationships, everywhere – you make people crazy in your own way. Things will rarely go wrong because of you and this is great. But you are a lot. You are wonderful in all those ways, but it's going to be a healthy thing for you and everyone else if you practice being a little chill like Dave. Take baby steps. Very small steps. Your head will blow up and the world might collapse if you do too much of this, especially in one go. Try to add the tiniest bit of spontaneity to your life. Also a bit of letting other people plan, even when the plan is vague or doesn't even exist yet. Try it. It'll be fine. Have a glass of wine. Take a nap. *Your* assignment is to learn to chill.

Chapter 24: You Made Your Point

You're in a meeting, heatedly pressing your brilliant, insightful point. You're right, of course, you know this. If only you could get all these dum-dums to see it. But they are just too slow. They don't get it. When do you give up? When do you just hush?

By the looks of it, you don't know.

You keep going; you keep arguing. Eventually they will get it, right? Nope. You irritate everyone and probably haven't changed anyone's mind. In fact, after a while, most people aren't even listening anymore. (Also, and I don't want you to stop reading when I say this, but it's remotely possible that no one is getting you because you are just all kinds of wrong.)

If this is one of your software features, people will avoid you. They won't want to work on teams or projects with you, and they won't want to be in meetings with you. People will start to avoid one-on-one time with you.

This sort of pressing of your point can happen anywhere. It can happen in meetings, one-on-one, with people on your team, anywhere, and outside of the office too.

If you have this tendency, you'll push your point with anyone who isn't getting it. Sometimes you get carried away and do it with your boss, a cop, a professor, or a judge. This rarely ends well.

First thing to do is check to see whether this is you. Because it could be, and you just might be in denial; thinking something like, "No, I am just explaining to the bridge trolls in my life the simplest things in the world."

This is a two-pronged approach. Start by looking for the behavior in someone else so you can really see what it looks like from the receiving end. Then talk to a few people close to you for some feedback. Ask carefully, or they might say you're not like that because they figure you'll just argue with them and tell them they are wrong. This is exhausting, and no one wants to do that with you. The best way to help make the conversation successful is to shut your pie hole and listen. Bite your tongue if you have to. Ask them, and then just listen. (See Chapter 28, Shut Up and Listen).

OK, now you might have a sense of whether this is you. What to do next? Dig into these two things: Do you just *need* to be right? Or is the problem maybe with your approach?

If it might possibly be because you need to be right – which is a whole book in and of itself – practice letting others be right. Practice listening. Practice trying things a different way. Take baby steps. Look for progress, not perfection. One of the keys to this effort is to sound real, to sound genuine, which is easier if you actually mean it.

I had a colleague who signaled when she gave up arguing with me. It was the phrase "Sure, fine, whatever." You can probably hear how that would sound. Pretty definite signal if you are paying the least bit of attention to anything but your own wonderful words. And I was just smart enough to hear it, take a breath, and listen.

Try asking for their thoughts. Try asking what they are *hearing* you say. Put this back on you, not them. Saying "I don't think I am saying this very well, let me try again," is way better than "How can you not see the answer is 43, you raging moron?"

When the person pressing the point is you, the second thing is to check to see whether the problem is your approach, not their stupidity. There's an old cult-classic movie called "This is Spinal Tap," which is a comedic mock documentary about a fading rock band. There's a famous scene where the guitarist explains to the interviewer that he had his amps custom-made so the dials went to 11, not 10. It was one louder than everyone else's. The interviewer basically says it's still the same dial turning, and the guitarist, who's not super bright anyway, doesn't get that point and thinks the interviewer isn't getting *his* point.

I've often thought of this one over the years when I am trying to get a point across to someone who is Just Not Getting It. It reminds me to stop saying the same thing, and no, saying it louder or slower is not different. It reminds me to try a different approach. Everyone's learning style is different.

How about: "You know, those amp dials all go from full-off to full-on. You could paint zero to one on there, or zero to 100. Doesn't matter. Still goes from all the way off to all the way on." Our fictional guitarist might not have gotten that approach, but it was different and worth a shot.

Now that we've dug into your psyche, let's dig into your topic a bit. This is big, so read it slowly:

How important is the point you're making?

I know, I know, everything you say is important, but really, *how* important? Because if it's not, just let it go. You are slowing the meeting down. You are killing the room. And if it really *is* important, try tabling it and coming back later, maybe one-on-one, when you – and everyone else – has time to settle down, and you can work on a new approach. Maybe even (gasp) assess whether you were wrong or whether your idea was dumb in the first place. It's possible.

Back to our guitarist. Let's say I tried, then tried a different way. And if he still didn't get it, then you assess how important it is (in this case, it is not at all), and then just move on. *Just move on.*

Learn to pick your battles. Parents know this well. Sometimes the kid went out in the world with clothes so mismatched that it hurt my soul. But hey, she was dressed. I won the battle I needed, just not all the battles. Think about whether whatever you are fighting for is really worth it.

Now that we've dug into your head, let's say *you* are wonderful, and when someone needs to hush, it's not you. What now? Try something like this: "I hear what you're saying, let me think about it and we can talk later. But I don't want to slow down our progress." Again, if it's not that important, let it go. If it needs to be worked through, then do it, but later. And use the same tools: Try a different approach. Seek to understand what they were trying to say. And Listen.

Chapter 25: Know When to Hush

I had a mentor who used to tell me to stop after the first sentence. It was great advice. There are many times we say something, and it's just fine. But all the words that come after the first sentence, the first thought, just ruin it. They dig you into that hole you then have to climb out of. "Hey, you look great!" (Stop there.) But what do we do? "I mean, because last year you were pretty fat." And it just gets worse as Jack tries to explain that it's all really a compliment because of the work you had to do to not be fat now.

I don't want the chapter on knowing when to hush to be the longest one, because some kinds of irony are not delicious. So let's try more of a summary style:

In the Weeds. Do you take everyone there? Watch for signs such as the boss cutting you off or seeming impatient. Or perhaps people are fidgeting or aren't paying attention (more than usual anyway). This often comes in two forms: too much detail (or too much focus on one detail), or a focus on something that's really about you and not relevant to everyone else.

The Sound of Your Own Voice. I first mentioned this in the chapter on meetings, but it bears repeating here: Some people feel like they need to say *something*. You don't. And don't say something someone else already said just because you think so highly of your version of the same idea.

Hairsplitting. This can drown a meeting and be irritating to others when you are arguing a small point that isn't really relevant and you're taking up a bunch of time doing it. Small points and details sometimes really do need to be clarified because they will make or break a plan. But you have to make sure that the one you are going on about is one of those. Otherwise, I think it's in the same family as Mansplaining and Needs to Be Right. Sometimes people split hairs because they were wrong on a larger point they just made and are trying, consciously or not, to save face; to be a little right. Or, like in Chapter 24, You Made Your Point, you just keep going because you *need* to be right.

Going On Too Long. Do you have a point? Get to it. Think about the high-level detail your boss and your peers might want to know, or at least, need to know. But that need rarely includes every detail in your work life since the last time you met. This is the same for friends and family.

Practice testing how brief you can be and still communicate what you need to get across. I would be at a table of managers, each going on and on about everything they were doing, you know, because they were all so awesome and important, and I would try to say something like "Everything's going well. We're in the middle of project X and are making good progress with everyone on schedule." That's it. If the boss or the other managers had questions, they could ask. It was an attempt to treat everyone's time with the respect it deserved. Just don't go too far and become the "everything's fine" person and not say anything useful at all (unless you truly have nothing to add).

Takes the Long Way to Get to the Point. A cousin of Going On Too Long. Also known as "short story long" – the unwanted flip side of "long story short." When you tell me about the delightful person you had coffee with this morning, you can skip the 30-minute soliloquy of every tiny detail in your life that brought you to that one moment. Really, you can. The story, at the level the rest of us care about, will be fine without all the detailed history. Make your point and save the rest for your journal.

I hold my hand up sometimes like I am fast-forwarding someone with a remote. I don't recommend this strategy, but you get the goal I have in mind. We just need a way that doesn't make you come across as a person I spend a much of this book trying to convince you *not* to be.

If you do any cooking, you might look at recipes from the web. I have noticed a pattern where there are often pages of story explaining everything in someone's life that made her need to write this recipe. And then finally, the recipe. It's so common that sometimes I actually see a "skip to recipe" link. I am incredibly grateful for this and often think that I need that in real life. Or you know that "skip intro" button we see in shows sometimes? That thing is a gift from heaven. I need it in my life too, not just on the TV screen. But again, when saying things like these, and I have, they can come across as mean or brusque, or like I don't care about what you're saying. We need a better way.

Part of that better way means to be patient and to put up with some of this from others. You're not perfect, and you've probably done some of these, so being tolerant – up to a point - with others is the Decent Human Being thing to do.

Try to develop tools to help you deal with this behavior. One way is seeking to balance the amount of background and detail with the value of the point you're getting to (hopefully soon). These are highly correlated. It still doesn't give you license to take everyone on a journey through your brain, but the more important the point, the more background can be useful.

Sometimes I try the gentle nudge. "OK, I understand this background pretty well now, thank you. Talk to me about X" (where "X" is the point you wanted them to get to). If it's a peer you know well or someone who works for you, giving feedback can help someone grow. But the saying about praising in public and criticizing in private holds true here.

It's a good idea to seek out feedback on how you come across in meetings and other environments. When I speak in public, my friends will ask how it went. I always say I have no idea. If I am watching someone else speak, I can tell you *exactly* how well they did or what went wrong. But when I am speaking,

I can't see it, so I really don't know. Feedback is important for improvement. Seek it. Accept it. Learn from it.

And learn when to hush.

Chapter 26: Read the Room

A good friend flew back home, somewhere in the far upper Midwest that doesn't need a name because no one cares about that empty wasteland. I think it's frozen 300 days a year, and they grow beets or something. She was going for her grandfather's funeral. A serious and sad occasion that for plenty of people is no time for humor.

For this family, there was tension about burial vs. cremation, and at some point she joked about looking on the bright side and bringing his ashes to Florida so he could visit where she lived. To everyone else, this was not funny. To her, it was. And to some people, a bit of humor during dark or sad times is healthy and helpful.

You need to Read the Room. This is a skill you need at work, whether in meetings or one-on-ones. This is a skill you need in life. Family and friends, spouses and partners, they all need this from you.

Some of you just aren't very good at it because you don't read social cues very well or you just aren't paying attention. If it's the paying attention part that gets you, well, so much of this book really comes down to encouraging and helping you to be a Decent Human Being. Much of this revolves around paying attention to something other than you.

If you just haven't thought about Reading the Room yet, or don't know how to begin, try starting here: Look for the tone of the conversation. Is it somber, quiet, tense, angry, anxious, sad, happy, excited, something else? Look at facial expressions for the same indicators. Let those guide you. The key is take it all in first, *before* you start running your mouth.

Like tone and expression, body language can be helpful too. Do people look relaxed or tense? Arms folded? Is someone or a few people sitting apart in a way that's unusual? If something is different, wait a bit to see what it feels like before you talk.

For those who don't read social cues well because you are on the end of the spectrum that often makes that difficult, that's a big and complex thing. But I can offer a little here about reading the room: Know that it matters. Know that you don't do it well. And then, because you are probably good at detail and planning, create a strategy to aid you. The simplest is to watch what others do and follow their lead. Not what that *one* guy does – no one likes him or his "wit" – but what the group in general seems to be doing.

Now think about *why* you are together. The topic of the meeting or gathering can be a good guide to your approach. This is also a good spot to make another pitch for you to stay on topic. If it's high-level stuff, stay there. Make notes for the detail stuff you want to dig into, but save it for a follow-up. And don't get into the weeds, wander off to something else because it's important to *you,* or worse, make it *about* you.

Next, consider *who* makes up the "audience" – the rest of the room. There was a day the family was sitting around reading, and one of my kids asked "Mom, who do you love?" And Mom immediately started listing the things she loves: "The moon, clouds, my book, the cat, dead trees…" Then she happened to look up and see eyes wide and mouths open from a husband and two children. "Oh yeah, and you people, of course," she added in what clearly was an afterthought. We ranked sixth. How about that? Know your audience. She maybe could have led with us first on the list as a courtesy.

Know your audience. I am super funny. Just ask me, I'll tell you how funny I am. But in my first job out of graduate school, the big boss had somewhere near zero sense of humor. Guess how well I handled that? Guess how long it took me to figure that Funny Boy was not funny? Way too long. You might already know the topic and tone, but knowing the people – their general personalities and dispositions – is important too. If you are light and they are serious, this often goes poorly. Same with snark, wit, humor, sarcasm, and all the other tools used by those of us who think we are Just. So. Clever.

And when it comes to humor, you *really* have to Read the Room. It's so easy to be tacky, crass, crude, or otherwise inappropriate in so many ways. This is a good place, after you've Read the Room, to also remember to Be You, Just Less (see Chapter 17). Dialing it back a bit is almost always a good idea. This is especially true if people consider you a personality that's "Big," or "Strong," or "Loud," or anything like those.

Like humor, cultural references are both wonderfully useful and at the same time, risky. We assume *everyone* has seen that movie, or knows the meme, or recognizes that character from the TV show. It can be effective to use themes and characters from popular culture to make a point. They are illustrative and if people know the reference, they will get it. It creates a sort of shorthand way to communicate a lot. But if they didn't watch "The Office," they won't get your perfect point made through your delightful reference to Michael Scott.

If you think about the bell curve, we know that *lots* of people have seen popular movies and series, but not everyone. And there's a huge variety in taste, plus our age tends to anchor our reference points. All this means that it can be a tough call when to use these references, so you have to know your audience. You have to Read the Room.

In personal relationships, Reading the Room is key to so many things. Important among them are knowing when to back off and when to stop. This might seem small, but it's not. You miss these cues and people get hurt.

It's also key when it comes to touching people, especially hugging them. This is directed mostly at the men, because we are usually the ones who get it wrong. We're not seeing the recoil. We're not seeing the flinch. We don't know when she lets it go because she doesn't want to come across badly or lose a step in the work environment.

There are lots of variations of this dynamic between gender and sexuality combinations, power imbalances, ages, and so on. But I choose to emphasize the one between men and women because there's so much lousy baggage we men bring to this one. It's the one that will have the biggest impact if we address it.

For touching, the easiest thing to do is *don't* (or at the very least, ask first). Refrain from touching other than ways that are in the fist-bump/handshake family. For hugs, that's more complex, because some people like to hug, and especially people they know well. For the men, here's a guide you can use: Let the other person lead. If she comes in for a hug, and you're good with that, hug back. If she comes in with a hand out, take it. Let her make the call. Easy.

In all the situations that Reading the Room matters, knowing your audience, knowing the tone, knowing the topic – it all gets at a singularly important idea: Context. Being who you are, and how you need to be, all comes down to that.

I don't mean you should be some sort of chameleon who changes with circumstance. This feels insincere. Not genuine. Think about it this way: You're a little different around your family than you are around friends or colleagues. Depending on where you are and with whom, it's entirely appropriate to both adjust the volume of you (Be You, Just Less), and the tone of you (Read the Room).

Chapter 27: Don't Fix Everything

There are two big reasons you should not try to fix everything: your time and everyone else's growth.

If you always fix it, if you always do the work, you will never be able to do more than just work. If you want to lead, to bring your influence to a bigger level, you have to let go of some things so you can do new things. You need the time.

And for others, they will never learn if you fix it for them. They can't grow if you fix it for them. They can't learn to solve problems if you solve the problems.

Here are the ingredients to *this* problem: We *know* how to fix it. And we want to be helpful. We want to show our skills and talents to the world. And it's just easier to do it ourselves most of the time, or at least that's what we mutter right before we do it.

We also don't want to ask people to do "our" work; even if it's not "our" work, it can feel that way to us. It can feel like we're imposing, or shuffling our work off onto someone else's shoulders. One of my friends calls it "throwing something over the wall," and it's not a good thing.

What to do then? For starters, it's a matter of resisting the temptation to just do it yourself. This takes practice and restraint. Ask them how they would approach the task, don't just tell them what to do. That's almost as bad as doing it. This might take less of your time, but it still inhibits their growth. Ask them for ideas and solutions. Talk with them; work with them until they get there, and then let them go do.

This approach can be frustrating and slow. But the reward is worth it. They grow, and you get time you can use to grow as well, and to move toward bigger responsibilities.

Managing that frustration, that impatience with the slow progress, is not the only challenge. You also have to constantly remember to adjust your timeline, to adjust your calendar, to accommodate the extra time this requires.

On top of this, you get to learn new perspectives: Your way is often not the best or at least, not the only way. And sometimes even when it *is* the best way, you need to allow their way because it's theirs, it's good enough, and they own it. (See especially the chapters on Listening, Teams, Taking a Back Seat, Leading, and Managing for more guidance.)

A happy side effect of this growth is it will reduce a gender dynamic dysfunction. For so many years men and women were taught, were trained, that men fixed things and that they solved the problems. Women were there to support, and they needed to be helped. As much as that narrative has faded, there are traces of it with us still, even if they are usually not conscious or knowingly linked to those past behaviors.

And when you layer on top that men were taught that this help, this fixing, was right, was proper, even chivalrous, this added another layer that made it harder to change a habit men might feel is just being polite. Add in all the time women were taught that they needed the help, or cynically, that they at least needed to *appear* that they did, so the fragile-ego men would be OK. When we throw on one more layer where men offering to help, to fix, to do, for women, is a way to "win" their attention and affection, then it gets even more difficult to change.

All this is to say that if you spend the time to develop yourself, and your people, in this way, even if they are peers and not people who work for you, it will be a good thing for society too. It brings us another step closer to treating women equitably, and it happens in this small way by you doing your job better and by creating the space for the people around you to grow.

Think past the workplace for a minute. Parenting, friendships, group activities, community involvement, and volunteer work, for example, are all places where this growth carries over.

This is another skill you need, everywhere in your life. Challenge yourself to master it. Don't Fix Everything.

Chapter 28: Shut Up (and Listen)

"Are you listening to me?" "No."

The only credit I get here is for honesty. Many of us might try to weasel and claim we were totally listening. Whatever; we weren't. Own it. Apologize and try again.

We learn to tune things out, especially as parents. There is so much noise coming from those little monsters, and sometimes they go on and on about nonsense. Tuning out is an important skill, but don't let it get away from you. It becomes a selfish way to live in your own world.

Listening well is a magical skill. In my coaching work, it's a big part of why things go well: People are heard. The focus is on them. It's powerful. It's not complicated to understand or all that difficult to do.

There's a broad stereotype that men are bad at this and women are good at it. Boys were taught that they should talk less and act more. They were taught to be decisive, to be quick. Girls were taught to listen, to care about others and what they have to say. Compounding this difference were structures that kept women from positions of intellect, power, and authority, so men viewed them as not worth listening to. (And yes, the irony of being the ones who kept women locked out was lost on the men.)

We've come a long way from the worst of that, and depending on your own experiences and on how sensitive your antenna is tuned for it, you might think it's all gone, still raging in the background, or somewhere in between. But the takeaway is to try to be in tune to your own tendency and adjust as needed. Most of us need to learn to talk less; some of us need to learn to talk more.

When listening well is your default mode, it doesn't matter the gender or anything else about the person talking, you are helping to make things better just by doing something that's good for your own life and your own career.

Paying attention to your speaker is what makes the difference. It means focusing on what they are saying, not on what you're planning to say next. It means you could actually repeat back what they said in a way that demonstrates understanding.

Take a brief look inward next time you're talking with someone. Are you just waiting until the sounds stop coming out of their mouth hole because they need to take a breath? If this brief silence is all you wait for as your signal to talk, you have a problem. And if you get together with a friend and all the best topics are about you, you're doing it wrong. Or you're just a jerk. Either way, room for improvement.

Practice listening. Practice making it about the speaker, not about you. Resist the temptation to tell the story about how you had the same exact experience, except yours was, of course, better and more interesting. Resist the urge to always steer the conversation back to you and whatever else besides you that you find interesting or important.

A powerful complement to listening is following up. It means *doing* something with that information. It's a wonderful signal that you heard them and cared enough to ask questions, to take action, to *do* something.

A side benefit to talking less and listening more is that you learn more. You already know all the stuff in your head. So shut up and listen.

Chapter 29: The Millennial Excuse

Most of the time I'm irritated by the use of "millennial." Lots of millennials probably are too. It has become a shorthand, a shortcut, a convenient label to put them all into a single bucket like they are some monolithic block of humans who are all the same.

There are two general uses of the term. One is for negative attributes: spoiled, lazy, self-centered, short attention spans, lousy work ethic, ruined by helicopter parenting, participation trophies, and an insane rat-race of competition for fewer and fewer winning slots in life. All sorts of things, none of them flattering.

Then there's the other use, the polar opposite about the "wonder" of the generation. They are all tech-savvy, progressive, "woke," diverse, and want to make a difference. All sorts of things, all of them new and improved over those who came before them. And it comes from within as they smugly tell everyone else how awesome they are, or from the outside as the previous generation marvels at "these kids today."

This is all a pile of crap. Millennials are, like every other group, a bell curve. They are individuals who cover a range of beliefs, attributes, and personality traits.

And the places we use The Millennial Excuse? When older generations want to dismiss them as flawed in some important way that the older generation, obviously, is not. And turned around, some millennials use the excuse to explain away anything in the world they don't want to learn, believe, or deal with. "Oh, we're not like that," says this millennial. "That's what our parents did, but we don't need to be polite or respectful, or follow tradition, those are dumb."

They are excuses in both directions.

Every generation for thousands of years thought it was hip and amazing and completely different. And every generation for thousands of years has been thought of by those before it as lazy, spoiled, and bound to end the world as we know it.

What's different now? Well, we've been labeling generations for a while now, and writing all sorts of thoughtful stories about them. And this one is recent. So we care more, and know more, about it. Also, everything new is, of course, better and everything old is, well, old, which is gross.

The group this label applies to doesn't even make sense in some ways. It, very generally, means kids who came of age at the turn of the century. But the common usage includes those born between 1981 and 1996. So someone who was 19 in 2000 is lumped in with the kid who was 4 in 2000.

This isn't the first generation to span what seems like an oddly long period. My Gen X includes people born in the mid-1960s all the way to those born in 1980. Very different groups at the beginning and end. So at best, these are mildly useful and mildly interesting conventions.

Millennials *have* dealt with enough technological change to basically upend society as we know it. It's hard to overstate how much this matters, how much we are all dealing with in a 24/7 completely connected world. This is important to understand if you want to have a clue, or some empathy, about their world.

If you're a Millennial, it's important to look at the attributes the world throws at you, and use them as checks. Looking at yourself in the mirror, see which ones apply to you. Be honest. Be real. The ones that are positive, that's great, they help you be a Decent Human Being. The ones that aren't, well, those are just "needs improvement" in the performance review of life. They are things you can work on as you grow, as you evolve.

And if you're the one sitting on the outside pointing fingers, stop it. You don't like it when we do it to *your* generation, so don't do it to theirs. And you better be nice, because the older Millennials are hitting that key age range where they are taking over. They are becoming the current crop of leaders, bosses, and decisionmakers.

Of course, we all have to deal with Gen Z. They don't have any power yet, except this one "little" thing: They are driving culture, fashion and taste. And we will like almost none of it, and they don't care even a little.

OK, enough about this. The Millennials already stopped reading. And since they did, and the Boomers are asleep, and no one thinks about the other generations at all, we can all agree that Gen X is better in every way.

Chapter 30: You Got Screwed

You really did. You got screwed. I can't overstate how important this is for you to recognize, and for all of us to remember.

Take your pick: Our world changed in 2001 when we were attacked here at home. The Dot-com bubble burst in 2002, the economy and markets tanked after 2007 when the housing market crashed. We spent much of this new century at war since the Afghanistan/Iraq invasions of 2001/2003. Hurricanes, floods, droughts, and fires wreak havoc around the country. Oh, and then the pandemic came in 2020 and crushed you, maybe again. Lives get upended. Plans large and small hit a wall of "NO!" And those are just the things that happened to millions.

For any one of you, there could have been an accident, an illness, a death of someone you love. There could have been something that took your dreams, told you to forget it, and to go get a crappy job so people around you can eat. Maybe your parents split up, or you got hurt badly enough that your dream of a sports scholarship vanished in a moment. The list goes on, sadly, and on.

The grumpy old men can tell you to buck up and just move on. But that's only part of it.

You, and the rest of us, need to acknowledge what happened. You need to be OK being angry or sad. You need to let yourself grieve for whatever you lost. Cut yourself a big fat break.

And when you've done all that, you have to let it go. Just let it go. You can't control what happened, but you *can* gain control in how you choose to let it affect you. It is power you can give yourself.

Letting it go might take time. It might take frustration, anger, tears, and pain. You'll need friends and family to help. Let them. Ask them if you need to.

If that's not enough, get professional help. It's worth it. Because if you don't let go of it, of the fundamental crappiness, the unfairness that life can deal any one of us at any time, it will eat you alive. It will crush you.

If you can't find a way to let it go, then for everyone else in your life, it will irritate, alienate, and eventually, push them away. This is bad; it's all bad.

Once you've given yourself space to hurt or be angry, and then you've let it go, it's time for the next step: Resilience.

You got screwed. Yep, you did. But what you choose to do next will define you. This is how we grow and get stronger. Maybe not the way we thought, or as who we thought we were, but our path changed. This is how it is now. So you start from there and make a new path. This isn't what you *wanted* to do, or what you *planned* to do, but resilience is about how we pick ourselves up and move on.

It sucks, and I'm sorry. It's been happening to people forever. Wars, famine, illness, natural disaster, things on a large scale and small. It still sucks for you.

So now what? What are you going to do? Give up and stay in bed until you rot?

Find a path. Find a way to start moving forward in your life, even if it's such a small step that it seems silly. Like taking a shower and putting on clean clothes. Do something.

Chapter 31: Who ARE You?

Being a Decent Human Being is a common thread throughout this book. For many chapters, my hope is the focus will help foster this as an added benefit; that it helps build it in you as a side effect. But often, already being a DHB is what makes the ideas in this book work.

As we close out Part II, let's take a step back to look at some overarching themes that can help: Emotional Intelligence, IQ, and personality profiles.

First up, Emotional Intelligence, or EQ. There's a ton out there, but start with Daniel Goleman's work. He's the one who brought it to mainstream consciousness.

The short version is that your capabilities in perceiving others' emotions – and relating to them – is a big deal. Same with your awareness of, and ability to manage, your own emotions, coupled with your level of social skill. These will make a profound difference in your success out in the world.

What does it matter? You show me a room full of engineers, and then show me the ones who have high levels of EQ, and I'll tell you where I'd place my bets on the future leaders, and the most successful engineers too. EQ is that important. It's probably obvious why these strengths would help you be a leadership and management success, but why would they help you be more successful at your profession, too?

You can be a great engineer, but if you the lack the skills to communicate what you are doing, what you need from others, and to translate what people say into what they really mean, then you will have a hard time getting the information from others to do your job well, and a hard time communicating to others the work you are doing. This weakness can have a significant cost to you in both directions.

When I was prepping for the exam to be a Certified Analytics Professional, there was a section on soft skills. It seemed like an afterthought to me at first, because it was out of place compared with all the other technical material. But the authors of the materials laid out a persuasive argument about being able to understand what your clients want, how to manage them, and how to communicate what you need and what you're doing. If you can't do that, often it won't matter how good you are at the data and analytics work.

Surgeons have a similar reputation to engineers. The typical criticism is that they don't have the bedside manner to communicate well with patients and often don't even seem to care about the human equation. What they care about is fixing the machine. Some people would argue that having an exceptionally skilled surgeon is the *only* thing that matters. The argument I make here is that the surgeon who also *can* listen, and actually cares about what the patient is saying, will likely have better outcomes over the long run. She is more likely to learn something relevant about a situation that would affect what comes next.

If you look at your awareness of others' emotions and your ability to manage your own, and find either lacking, these are great places to focus to make your future better and your life easier. There are plenty of resources a web search away that you can do on your own, with a coach, or through coursework.

And if you don't see any weak areas, it might be worth getting a second opinion. Ask your mother, she'll tell you (unless you have that mother who thinks you are the greatest thing to ever grace the planet. Yeah, don't ask her). Ask a friend or a colleague who will be candid with you.

Now let's talk about intelligence or IQ. It's one of the places my favorite equation comes into play: Standard Deviation – and the bell curve. IQs are "normed," they are standardized so that the average IQ is 100. If you look at a bell curve, it shows you that 50% of the country is there or below. This is important to let that sink in because it matters for you in the world and at work.

Half the country has an IQ that means they are somewhere between unable to live independently and can boot a laptop as long as nothing goes wrong. Half. This should serve as a general reminder of why things often are the way they are. It also can help remind you to remember your audience. There's a sweet spot between talking over someone's head and talking down to them. And it's often hard to find. We all need to remember though, that IQ is inherent and not learned. So wherever someone falls along that bell curve is just who they are, and like skin color, not something we should judge people by.

Try using this as a guide: Interact with others as simply as you can given the subject matter. But don't dumb it down right out of the gate, especially based on appearances or other assumptions. You'll get burned by this – a lot. If your listener needs some clarification you might get follow-up questions, or you might sense it. Then you can explain more. This will help keep you from insulting someone, or hurting their feelings. Plus it will help you talk less, and stay inside others' attention spans, too.

When my wife was just out of school and out on her own, she had a mechanic who would talk to her like she was an adult. It's easy for technical people like him, from a generation before, to assume young people, especially women, don't know anything about cars. And it might even have been his experience in general. But he treated people like they were grown-ups and then explained whatever they wanted to know; whatever follow-ups they had. She appreciated that, and trusted him.

All this said, your peer group is probably not representative of the whole. Let's assume most of the people around you went to college. That means they are probably all on the other side of the 50% line, the other side of that 100 IQ. The same logic – and the same advice applies. But the new reference range is somewhere between "made it through college, barely," and "so much smarter than you are they don't even know how to talk to you."

Another way this affects you is part of perspective and bias I talk more about in Chapters 46 and 58. We typically assume other people are like us. We just assume, unconsciously, that they've seen the movies we have, understand the cultural references we do, and appreciate the same things we do. If you were designing a logo or some elements of a marketing campaign, for example, are you making something pleasing to you and your peer group, or to the group you are targeting? You have to think this through because your customers might not be like anyone in your office. Another sneaky little bias is when we design things to show our peers, bosses, or award judges just how clever we are. Sometimes when I read an academic paper, I get a sneaking feeling the researcher was showing off how well *they* understood something that was super esoteric. Or that they used methodologies that were far more fancy and complex than needed for the given question.

Have you ever looked at some advertising and thought "Dang, that's really dumb"? Take a step back and look at the product. Maybe the target market is broad and needs an appeal that doesn't lose too many people. (Although maybe it *was* just dumb.)

IQ also affects you directly. Knowing where you land on the IQ bell curve can help you see what's in your wheelhouse easily, what's a stretch, and what is outside your range. Unless you are a savant at something, your IQ does and should limit you, and guide you to things you'll be good at. Or maybe you are more average, but have amazing visual motor skills or perceptual reasoning abilities. You could be a fantastic mechanic or interior designer, but a lawyer? Not so much.

The higher your IQ, the harder it will be for you to sustain repetitive or basic tasks, for example. And the more toward average you are, the harder advanced professions will be (not to mention the training to get there). This doesn't mean you can't or shouldn't reach. It just means that being honest with yourself means you will know your limits and leave some things alone. This can save you a lot of frustration. And it means the ones you go for, the ones that are a stretch, will be harder for you and require a lot more work. Just know that and be prepared for it, and try not to be so irritated at the ones the same work seems to come so easily to.

The last thing for this chapter is personality profiles. There are some great tools out there to help understand and evaluate your personality, and some that are probably not so good too. And when you get the results of these assessments, brace yourself for lots of high-minded pronouncements and attempts to make the wording technical and scientific. But look for big-picture ideas and measure these against how you perceive yourself. A tool that brings some clarity to who you are and how you work best can be powerful.

Indicators about introversion and extroversion, for example, or how well you work alone, or in groups, can tell you a lot about you. Some people perform wonderfully just plugging away in a spreadsheet all day, and some people would rather have a fingernail pulled than do that. These assessments can help guide you down a path of leadership or one of professional work excellence and achievement.

A caveat though: Like IQ, don't let these define you or put you in a box of your own making. Use them as a guide, a tool, to help you along your journey. Introverts, for example, can do large and loud things, it's just harder and requires a careful attention to quality recharge time. These things don't define you; you do.

Personality, IQ, and EQ are tools; they are pieces of knowledge and information you can use to help find your path – and to travel it well. They can help you answer: Who ARE You?

PART III: Just No

It does not matter what kind of person you *think* you are. You are defined by what you say, what you do, how you act, how you treat others. These show the world who you *are*.

Some things, like the clothes we wear, are individual preferences. You can argue all day long that it's "your choice," "your style," that "fashion is inherently subjective." And I would say, "Yes, that's all true."

You could argue that "it doesn't matter what's on the outside," and I would also agree. But I'd still say you are missing the point that's relevant here: People don't know what's on the inside. They judge by what they see.

And they judge by what you say and what you do. If you act selfishly, if you appear shallow, mean, or ignorant, then that's who you are to the world. If you create that perception, it largely doesn't matter whether it's true or not.

In these chapters, I encourage taking a wider view of your personal, individual, and subjective choices. I encourage that you consider how you appear and how you act in this context: You are part of society, part of our human system. Whether you like that or not, you are.

Knowing this, knowing that it matters, can help guide you to adjust accordingly. When they align – the cover and the inside – the world can see who you are inside by looking at the outside. This leaves plenty of room to be you; but in a way that more or less fits with where you want to go, and what you want to accomplish, in the world.

I will also argue in these chapters that some things are not really choices. Well, they are, but it's a choice between being a Decent Human Being or not. That's the position I take here, and am willing to defend on behalf of society's collective wisdom (hopefully not just my own feelings), and to say "Just No."

All that said, there are chapters here – and all over this book – that might make you feel picked on, like you aren't good enough, or that your choices are being criticized in a biased or subjective way.

Don't give up or put the book down in frustration or irritation. You are not a failure if you don't do, live, or believe everything in here. Your choices are most definitely yours to make – not mine, or anyone else's.

Remember to take it as a guide to use, often a mirror to hold up, so you can decide what's right for you, where you are just fine, and where you could do a little better.

And use it as a tool to help you deal with everyone else; to get along better with all of those wonderful, annoying, maddening, and amazing people in your life.

Chapter 32: Don't Be an Ass

There are certain professions and certain personality types that are sticklers for accuracy and detail. They value knowledge, reason, logic, and rational thinking. Years ago, it was assumed this was a male trait and that women were not suited for such thinking. So women of course couldn't be engineers or doctors or pilots or whatever. Obviously, it was the men saying those things. Women spent a century or two proving otherwise, and in many ways, still are having to prove it.

My gut instinct was to label this idea of being an ass as a male trait. I even had this chapter titled "Don't Be a Dick" for most of the drafting process. I still believe it's mostly men, especially when it comes to the worst of the behaviors, but I wanted to get away from a gender-specific term.

This chapter starts with the "stickler" professions because there's a line between prizing accuracy and reason, and being an ass. And far too many people don't know where that line is.

So let's see whether we can help draw the line.

If you are one of our "Sticklers" for accuracy, precision, and detail, then the key for you is *how* you do it. Because those things *are* important, they help balance out the Daves of the world, the poor planners, the sloppy thinkers (see Dave's story in Undisciplined Thing, Chapter 23). Without our Sticklers, the world would fall apart. Dave waves his hand and says we'd all be fine, but that's only because the pilot is a stickler and makes sure the plane lands – and Dave doesn't think about that at all.

Mansplaining, condescending, patronizing, insulting, belittling, bullying – so much of the Stickler comes off this way. Figuring out how to say things kindly, gently, and in a supportive and helpful way is what matters. Also doing a little internal pre-check can be helpful to make sure you're really adding something to the conversation, that you're moving an issue forward.

It's also more likely that your message will be heard. And because so often this is male behavior toward women, getting this communication right helps remove an ugly layer of sexism too. Whether you are a Stickler or not, watch for these behaviors in yourself and beat them back with a stick, firmly.

Branching out from the Sticklers, part of curbing this tendency – with the goal of making your ass a body part and not your personality – is to figure out *why* you are doing it. Showing off, consciously or not, is probably the biggest reason.

Men can fundamentally be peacocks and want to show everyone how strong, talented, or smart they are. The companion to this lovely trait is making sure people feel stupid, that you know little, so that they feel even more superior.

And to boost that feeling of superiority, another way they can be a giant ass is by criticizing, by tearing down others. Sometimes this is a companion to the patronizing family of behaviors, but often it's employed alone. It's used just so they can feel bigger, stronger, more attractive, and generally better than those around them.

This drive for superiority often comes as criticism, as ridicule, of what someone is wearing, looks like, says, does, believes, thinks, eats, dreams of, you get the idea – it's of anything. You will attack what they say. It's like a power charge in a video game. You beat them down, drain them, and charge yourself with it.

Another trait to look for in yourself that can drive this behavior: Straight-up jealousy. Sometimes you don't even know that's what's driving you, but it makes you basically crap on other people's success. You attribute whatever good that happens to others as luck, connections, family resources, anything but their own work and talents.

Also watch for when you make assumptions about motivation or intent, when you jump to conclusions, especially assuming the worst of reasons in what others do or say, while you expect everyone else to assume the best when it comes to you (a common type of bias).

If you're guilty of any of these, if you're not sure, or even if you're convinced this isn't you at all, there's a solid strategy we all should use: If you don't have something nice to say, don't say anything at all. This old saying is wonderful advice. It's also the best way to train yourself not to be an ass. It helps you learn to listen first, to think about what you're going to say next, and why.

I want to emphasize here that you really need to stop and think about what you were going to say. Actually play it in your head first, and if it's not supportive, kind, and positive, don't say it.

This strategy will help you be a better person, and it will help you grow as a mentor, as a leader, as a teacher. It holds true at work, at home, in relationships, and as a parent.

Think about being a co-worker, a friend, a mentor, a teacher, a partner in a relationship, a parent. How *should* you treat anyone? Being a gentle guide so the person on the other side of the conversation can get there themselves is magical. Try to picture when someone was an ass to you, and think about how it felt. Don't make the people around you feel this way.

The service organization Rotary uses what it calls the Four-Way Test as an ethical guide. It reads:

"Of the things we think, say, or do: Is it the truth? Is it fair to all concerned? Will it build goodwill and better friendships? Will it be beneficial to all concerned?"

The Four-Way Test is a great guide to personal and professional relationships, but there is another saying that I like even more, especially as it ties into the ideas in this chapter:

"Before you speak, ask yourself: Is it true, is it kind, is it necessary?"

While the saying appears in slightly different forms and is attributed to various authors, it is powerful, simple, and elegant. If you keep this in your head and your heart, you will be a better human.

Is it true, is it kind, is it necessary?

Chapter 33: Are You a Dark Cloud?

Every time you're in a meeting – in any group setting really – it seems like there's always that one person. He covers the light in a Dark Cloud. She brings the rain to the parade. Every. Time.

Your idea is stupid. It won't work. It's too much work. There's not enough time. We don't have enough people. We don't have the budget for it. She's too busy to add more work; his current workload is much more important.

This negativity is the first thing out of her mouth. And he's the first one to speak up most of the time. Way to set the tone, Cathy. Way to be a buzzkill, Dan.

Potential roadblocks, pitfalls, and other unhappy possibilities absolutely should be discussed and considered, solutions sought. But when it's always negative, and always the first thing – that's the problem. It colors everything that comes next. It kills the energy in the room and whatever excitement there might have been for the topic. This is a problem for the leader, and for everyone who has to suffer through it.

And it's a problem for the person doing it. Cathy and Dan get reputations. No one will want them on their teams. We start avoiding them.

How do you manage the Dark Clouds? The biggest bang for your buck is to anticipate that negativity and to be ready for it. When it happens in a group setting, shut it down and redirect gently. "Hey Cathy, let me jump in here. It's great you are thinking about where we might run into problems. I want to get through fleshing out this idea first, and then we'll come back to what we need to watch out for."

Be kind and positive. Every time. Even when they are not. It does get old. It can be frustrating. It will get to you. This makes it harder to avoid getting angry, losing your temper, or even speaking harshly. It means you have to remind yourself to keep *You* in check too, and that it takes effort to manage their negative behavior.

Make sure you *do* go back and have "problem time." It shows that you weren't just shutting them up, which would beat them down and send a signal that you don't really care what they had to say. And it's valuable to anticipate problems and look for solutions, so ignoring your buzzkills loses that insight – insight you might have very much wished you had when something you *could* have managed screws up everything later on.

Sometimes circumstances dictate that you address the concern right then and there. Whether that's the case, or whether it can wait until a better time, when it *is* time to address it, ask them for specifics; ask for details of their concerns. Often they make blanket statements that when you probe a bit, they withdraw the grumble because it turns out that's all it was: just a grumble.

As a manager, try assigning an official "Poke a Hole in This Idea" role each time to someone different. It would be their task, when it's time to go there, to lead off that discussion, to spark it with that first worry. "What could go wrong; what aren't we seeing; where is the risk?" Assigning that role can reduce the burden of appearing negative on a person. And if you are the one whose thoughts always go dark, it'll be an approved window for you to voice your concerns.

Taking a bigger view is helpful too. If it's a pattern, talk to your Dark Cloud in advance, one on one. Sit down and tell them you appreciate how they tend to see the holes; the things that could go wrong. Make sure they know you think it's important. Then talk to them about not leading with it, about letting the conversation bloom a bit before getting into what's wrong or could go wrong. When you make sure they know they are heard and valued, and when you enlist them to be part of the strategy, not just to shut them down, you can make a lot of progress.

This can be part of a bigger-picture conversation about whether that person is happy in the organization. I have had this conversation, and good things can come from it. They can start to see the impact of the trait and realize how serious it is to the group and to their future. They see that they need to rein it in because they really do like their job and the organization.

Sometimes the conversation brings it out in the open that they are just not happy. It can be powerful to get that out in the open; to put words to those feelings. Because then you can work with them to see whether you can fix it together, or whether they need to look for something else.

What if *you're* the Dark Cloud? What if you recognized something in this chapter about you? Start with looking for the "why."

Are you typically cautious and reactive? Are you resistant to change or uncomfortable with it? Is it just where your mind goes in the face of a new idea? If your intent truly is to be helpful, then stop to think about how you do it. If all you really want is to make sure everyone sees the problem before it's too late, then try just not going first. It can be as simple as that. Maybe the better window is a little deeper into the conversation, or maybe someone else will sling the dark arrow this time.

Leading off with darkness casts a shadow over everything that comes next. Let the idea build enough so that the concerns you have are things to work through, not just a reason to kill the idea before it has a chance to grow strong enough to survive the challenges.

For the person who is reactive by nature, or just generally pessimistic, we can work on that. Harness it. Put it to good use where it makes sense, and keep it in check in other places. Work on *how* to say things. Try using questions, not statements. Look to explore an idea and let the flaws show themselves instead of assuming it's all bad and wrong. Seek an approach that's gentle, positive, and supportive.

But what if your trait is of a different sort? Some people just want to look super smart by poking a hole in the idea. They feel stronger by cutting other ideas (and people) down. This one is harder to admit, because it's not very pretty. But if you see any of it, or even suspect it, make sure you were paying attention in Chapter 32, Don't Be an Ass. Might be best if you re-read it. Or read it for the first time if you skipped it because you already *knew* that you weren't an ass.

Another trait to manage is cynicism. We see it all too often, in and out of the workplace. The cynics are just delighted to weigh in on why something *really* happened, what the *real* motivation was, and it's never for a good reason.

I knew a great editor who always counseled journalists to be skeptical, not cynical. Skepticism helps you do a better job; it helps you ask the right questions. It's healthy in reasonable doses.

But cynicism is corrosive, it beats people down. Cynicism is not cool, not a badge of honor. It's cliché and predictable to watch the cynics dump on anything people say that's positive or happy.

Look up in your world; check for the Dark Cloud. And whether it's above your head or someone else's, do something about it.

Chapter 34: Don't BS

When I was all of 19 and going through lots of training in the Marine Corps, most of it was led by corporals and sergeants who seemed super grown up and knowledgeable. The reality was that most of them were not much older than I was. And most of them didn't know a whole lot more about the subject at hand than whatever was in the training materials we had in front of us.

But there was something they did that has stuck with me all these years. If you asked a question that they did not know how to answer, they would say something like "Well that's an outstanding question Private. I do not know the answer, but I *will* find out and get back to you."

What was different about this, different than the experiences I have had since then, is they didn't BS their way through it to avoid looking dumb. They didn't give me some answer that sounded good, one that I wouldn't have known whether it was correct or not.

The next thing that was different is that they *always* got back to you with an answer, even if it wasn't much. But they tried, and they followed up.

This might appear so basic, so obvious, as to not warrant a chapter, but this isn't how it goes most of the time. We all know it.

People don't want to look dumb, and there are all sorts of dynamics at play here. Men always have an answer, right? So they let their range drift all the way to guessing and wrap it in some air of intelligence. Bosses often don't want to seem like they don't have all the answers.

I actually had a boss who once told me flat out that she couldn't admit that she was wrong because it would make her look weak. This knocked me back a bit. It was hard to process and hard to imagine her being OK with this. How could you let something wrong go uncorrected just because you didn't want to look bad? How bad were you going to look when it came out later anyway?

It dawned on me years later that because she was a woman managing a lot of people who had a lot of brainpower, she was probably dealing with sexism in ways I hadn't considered. It was still the wrong approach for a leader, but in that context, it went from something that made no sense to me, something that seemed like just lousy management, to something that cut deeply into the way things still are. It revealed more about the structures and the legacies that plenty of women in the workplace are still dealing with on top of actually doing their jobs.

And this point of view probably extends to anyone who worries about coming across as weak, or without answers or knowledge because of youth, inexperience, race, gender, ethnicity, or disability – you name it. It might feel even more important to seem knowledgeable in an effort to blunt biases that others have. Sorry. It sucks, it's an extra burden, and it shouldn't be that way. But you still shouldn't fake it. Try to find another way.

For all of us, whatever the reason we avoid saying we don't know, try a version of what those corporals would say. "Great question. Let me get more info on that and get back to you," and then just keep moving. No weakness, no failure. Just good leadership. Just being an effective part of the team.

You could even throw it out to the group like: "Great question. Who has some ideas about this?" Just remember to accept what's offered as input, not fact. You still need to add in the "… let me get more info on that and get back to the group" part.

Just don't BS. It will show. People will see it, and they will think less of you. And you will have earned it.

Chapter 35: Social Media

Why do you use social media? I know that's a wildly broad question. Which platform(s) you use is a big question alone. And then there's the "how" and the "why" for each one.

Your age, gender, personality, profession, and interests all are big drivers of which platforms you use, how you use them, and how often. Let's make this easier by ignoring *which* platform you use and focusing on the "how" and the "why."

Is it to find out what's going on in the world? To keep up with what's happening with your friends and family, and to share your life's changes with them?

Maybe you like to follow trends, styles, or personalities, or keep current on the latest stories and memes? Or maybe it's just purely for entertainment?

Whatever the combination, social media can be interesting, helpful, fun, entertaining, connecting. It is where much of our shared cultural world comes from and is fueled by. And the platforms make staying connected a whole lot easier (and more likely) than trying to write a letter. (I know, I know, what's a letter? You're funny.)

What motivates you beyond these? The quieter, darker things that you don't acknowledge out loud, maybe not even to yourself? Is it to show the world how amazing your life is? Is it habit? For validation? Just something to do, something to pass the time?

For the pieces that matter here, we'll tackle it in three parts: How it affects your personal growth, your outlook, and your job.

All that you experience on social media platforms can help you grow as a human. In a way, it's another library that's just waiting to be explored, waiting to expand your mind and open you up to new possibilities and ideas. What's important here is what you're exploring and how much.

Think about it like whatever you're streaming on TV. You can be mindlessly entertained for hours on end, days even, with trashy content that's fun. Or you can watch serious documentaries and lots of shows about how things are built or done. And in the middle are plenty of shows and movies that aren't quite so serious, but still thought-provoking and interesting. What's your balance in all of this?

It's the same with social media. The advice is like what we hear about eating: Everything in moderation, find balance, and don't wallow in junk too much. The flip side to all the amazing potential is simple: You can spend all your time in it, which comes at the expense of all the other things you could be doing that would bring value or happiness to your life.

When it comes to your outlook, this is about how your social media consumption affects you. If it wears on you because much that you see seems filled with people who are better looking than you are, more "together," or with what looks like the resources to play and live like the elites do, then this is another cost beyond your time.

It can make you feel lousy about your own life, even when your life is just fine. It might help to ask yourself whether your friends on social media are "real" ones who you actually connect with, or whether they are a collection of humans there for your entertainment.

And then let's talk about social media and your work. First off, avoid posting or scrolling at work. Aside from wasting time your organization pays for, it, at the very least, looks bad to others, and gives your boss a lousy impression of your work ethic.

Don't assume your stuff is private. Most of us probably don't look at our own profiles from the view someone else sees, especially as someone who isn't connected to you. Often, outsiders can see enough. And easily enough, something we meant for our smaller circle of friends gets passed along to someone you'd rather have not seen it.

Fair or not, people will judge you by what they see on social media, so you should consider how it looks. If you want to get hammered, maybe don't post that photo of you half-dressed, with sloppy drunk face, sticking your tongue out while throwing some "gang" sign. You look silly in pretty much any context except maybe if you have friends who are 20. But they are 20 and don't know squat.

Then when you consider the things you share, "like," or pass along: that content defines your outlook to others. So if it's ignorant, sexist, or racist, then that's how people will view you. While some of the ways people judge you aren't fair, these will be.

Another dimension beyond appearing trashy – or just as a bad person – are the elements that reveal other aspects of your personality. Do you focus on money and status? Do you show off? Do you come across as a narcissist where everything is about you and how wonderful you are? Do your attempts at being humble become thin wrappers around bragging?

When you post or comment, take to heart the advice in the chapters on Mansplaining (don't), Don't Be an Ass (also don't), and Attack the Message (not the messenger). And please resist the temptation to turn whatever someone posts into something about you. Be happy for whatever your friend just shared, and don't use it as an opportunity to talk about when that same thing happened in your life (only better).

One last thought: Let's talk about expanding your "personal brand." I hear that a lot. If you're working in the world of social media – or one that is highly dependent on it – and your "brand" matters, of course you need to manage it well. (This is even more important if you are trying to monetize your brand, but that's a wholly different topic.) And you can also make a reasonable argument that managing your brand is a bit like keeping your résumé polished. It's part of how the world knows you, and you want it to be your best foot forward. Those make sense to me, but the caution I feel is when this is really just an excuse to be a narcissist who spends half the day getting poses and scenes just right and posting them. To what end?

Plus, spending all this time creating and curating an image of You means you are spending the time building a reality show of yourself that isn't actually real. When you are running the reality show of You, you are working, not living.

Instead, you are getting the scene just right for the photo or video, not actually taking in the scene around you. You are staging the shot of you at the museum, the concert, the restaurant, the mountains, but you didn't really soak up the art, the music, the food, or nature. The photo was important to add to your reality show, but you neglected to experience life along the way.

Use social media to learn, to grow, to connect and stay connected. Use it for fun, for entertainment. Use it in moderation, and let it be part of what makes you healthy and a Decent Human Being.

Chapter 36: Don't Be Stupid

Have you ever run into that teenager who doesn't seem to know anything at all about the world? Maybe they know plenty about video games, or TikTok, or whatever they find interesting at the time. But as far as pretty much anything else is concerned? Nada. And they don't seem to care that much about it either.

You probably mostly write that off as a thing about teenagers that's pretty common and maybe even normal for a lot of them. And you move on. Maybe you smile a little to yourself or shake your head.

It feels very different when you run into someone like that who is a grown-up; someone who doesn't really seem to know anything, or care to learn. And it doesn't seem to bother them that they don't know anything.

I mean, sure, we meet people who don't have the same cultural or generational reference points, and that can require some re-thinking, some translating, to relate, but that's different.

With the completely clueless, the happily ignorant, it's weird. If this is you, even just a little; if you say things like "I don't care about any of that, because it doesn't affect me and it's not relevant to my life," then let me argue otherwise.

Make an effort to understand the world. I don't mean that you need to spend all your time learning and caring about things that maybe you really don't. But a passing familiarity with a range of topics will go a long way.

Let me throw out just a handful of reasons:

- It's your obligation in a civil society to be informed
- The more you know about the world, the more everything will make

sense

- You will be more interesting to others, and you will find new experiences and ideas that attract your attention
- It will make you smarter, more functional, more useful to the world and to yourself
- It will increase your confidence to handle the world and all that it *will* throw at you
- It will broaden and deepen your perspective and awareness, and help bring more balance to your outlook.

Here are a few steps you can take:

- Read a book. When you finish one, read another one. Whether it's getting through a page a day or a book a week, doesn't matter
- Subscribe to a few newsletters – and actually read them. They take just a few minutes. Pick one that summarizes news and current events, then another one about your industry, and then a third about your profession. Maybe throw in one more about random interesting things
- Listen to people around you and ask questions about whatever didn't make sense or sparked a thought
- Whenever you have a life task in front of you, search for some "how-to" articles or go check out a YouTube video on how to do it. Even if you decide that you'll pay someone else to do it, you now have some background that will enable an intelligent conversation and, more likely, an efficient transaction.

Take just a little time to work on that curiosity muscle. A few minutes a day. That's all it takes. You'll thank yourself later and so will everyone else.

Chapter 37: You're Wearing That?

Boys wear shorts. Men wear pants. You can wear your shorts to work out, or at the beach, or wherever you *should* wear shorts. But they are not a replacement for pants, no matter how nice they are. You look like a child. Stop it.

And for the women? Tights are *not* pants. Yoga pants are not pants. You just went outside with pantyhose on and forgot to put on a skirt. You are basically naked from the waist down. We can see everything.

Oh and there's more, so much more, in the World of Chuck: No hats backward, excepts for welders, catchers and boat pilots ("But there are others!" the Mansplainers cry out. Yes, I know, but you get the idea).

Take your hat off indoors. Camo is for soldiers and maybe hunters (and only when soldiering or hunting), not for civilians. On anything else? Just no. Slides are not shoes, and don't even mention them with socks. Columbia makes shirts to fish in, not wear out to dinner. Also, hoodies, a T-shirt, and jeans might be your go-to look. It's easy, requires little thought, says you aren't interested in fashion, and is comfortable and safe. But as a style, it's a borderline cop-out. Make sure it's not all you know, all you have, and that you can dress for occasions where that outfit doesn't make sense. Be able to dress like an adult.

While we're here, how about you ditch the slides and the Crocs? I mean, sure, Crocs are great for the garden or for working in places like hospitals and restaurants, but they do not *look* good. That's not their point. The trend to use them in fashion is a great example: Just because a celebrity, model, or fashion "influencer" wears them paired with real clothes, sometimes covering the Crocs in kitschy adornment, doesn't mean *you* can pull that off. It matters. You have to be honest with yourself and make sure it works. Mostly, when we adopt the odd fashion trends, we just look silly.

Same with slides. I started seeing them on high school kids, mostly boys, coming out of some athletic practice. Almost always with socks on. We can cut them a break because that's not fashion, that's ditching the cleats for something to get you home.

Then they spread like a virus and they're everywhere, trying to become a normal piece of footwear. Like Crocs, slides have their practical uses for sure. But widespread use doesn't mean it's a good look for you in the time and place you're wearing them. It might be sloppy and lazy. Look in the mirror and be real with You.

My "Just No" list is endless, but that's not important. What *is* important is to use the stuff for what it's intended. Dress appropriate to your age and to the occasion, to the time of day, time of year, and to the task at hand. Also, and I shouldn't even have to say this, did you *look* in the mirror before you left? And that includes the view from behind. You can do it.

Style, you might be fuming, maybe even out loud, is subjective, it's personal. And what if I just don't care about style? And what the hell do you know anyway, Mr. Book Author?

Yes, this is all true. But it's beside the point. The point is that you can do whatever you want; wear whatever you want. You are free to do that. Please, oh please curb your indignation long enough to really *hear* that. Because I mean it.

Though you do need to wear pants, not tights (stop yelling at the page). And lay off the leopard print too.

And for some of you, your questionable fashion choices are really "anti-fashion" statements. You are intentionally pairing socks and sandals, and generally rocking a look that might seem like you slept in a bus station. You are deliberately signaling that you don't care about mainstream fashion and have no interest or need to conform to standards set by others. This makes me proud to see. But this chapter is still for you. Bear with me and see why.

Anyway, for all of you, now it's your turn. Take all of my rants, my preferences, my opinions, and toss them out. Now replace them with your own views about style. Unless you don't have any views on it, then trust mine.

Seriously, commentary aside, you can wear whatever you want. And I support your choice, your taste, your freedom. And you absolutely don't need my blessing or to care about my opinion. I am not saying any of that. What I *am* saying is your freedom is not free. Those choices have consequences.

What you wear is like what you say, what you do, how you act, and what you post on social media: It is how people decide who you are.

I am arguing that you should make these choices with full knowledge of this, not just that you rock that look, or that you don't care because you are fierce and independent (or because you are a sloppy-ass dude who doesn't care).

The easiest way to do this is to stay appropriate within context. If you do that, you don't have to think about it too much.

And if you want to show your style, do it by pushing the bounds of that context *some,* not a lot.

If you really *want* to go all out and just be some wild, loud version of you, be ready for the baggage that comes with it.

You don't have to care what people think, but that doesn't mean you won't be judged. You have to be willing to accept the consequences of that.

Think about it like tattoos, piercings and hair. What is considered "normal" and "acceptable" has shifted a great deal in recent years. I mean, in the time between when I started and finished this book, I might have already lost the yoga-pants battle, and maybe the one over Crocs too. But most of us have a sense of the boundaries for the world we expect to live in. You keep it within that, or you seek roles where no one cares that you have a face tattoo, or a dozen piercings, or a beard that's braided and colored into a rainbow. (Yes, I am looking at you, Mr. Barista.)

If you don't look right for the sandbox you play in, then you need to change, find another sandbox, or push the boundary and live in the sandbox where you stand out, and deal with what comes from that.

Dressing poorly or inappropriately given the environment makes you look ignorant or uncaring, sometimes even disrespectful. Most of you wouldn't show up to a friend's wedding in your best fishing shirt and a hat on backward. (Unless that was the theme I suppose. 'Merica.)

A few tips that can help: Look for earth tones, muted colors and solids. Use a color palette that plays off your skin tone. The darker the skin tone, the more you can branch away from the earth tones into stronger, brighter colors. Look for "just right" in sizing. I know it's a big ask and can be hard to do, but when clothes are too tight, they look wrong. When they are too loose, they look wrong. You do not look good.

Go for quality, not quantity; go for fewer, better pieces. Think about combinations; think about accessories.

Own a tuxedo, and have it fitted. Your last rental should be your prom. Or own a perfect Little Black Dress. Or both. You do you.

There are so many things about style that vary across cultures, ethnicities and regions, so if there are things from your background that are important to you, find ways to integrate them. Show them proudly, but within the context of where you are and what you are doing.

And for the love of god, get the suit tailored. When your sleeves are too long, you look like you're wearing your parent's clothes, not yours, like you are playing dress up. Having a smaller wardrobe lets you focus on getting each piece just right, and it helps target most effectively how you spend the money you can dedicate to this.

Watch the most tasteful and fashionable around you. They probably don't wear a bunch of loud colors and patterns. How do the people you look up to dress? Learn from them. Look at those you admire in your profession and take some clues from what they wear.

Even if you're the person who just doesn't care that much about what you wear – and that's OK, I'm not trying to change that – I am pushing you to pay attention just enough to do the minimal things well.

Think about whether the style fits *you,* not just one that looks good on a model. I have seen capris *actually* look good on a man. But they fit well and didn't look like calf-length baggy cargo shorts, which in case you are wondering, is never a good look.

It all comes down to "looking right for the part," and here, that's about context, about time, place, and role.

All of this so far is about the cover of your book. Inside matters too. Feeling good in what you are wearing is powerful.

When something fits right, when you look in the mirror, and go "yeah, that works *nicely,*" you feel better. You walk taller; your confidence grows a bit. These are good things that can be had by anyone who makes a little effort, who takes a little time, to be good to themselves.

You can be you, you can be expressive, you can be individual. But while you do all of that being you, you can still pay attention to context. And please, whatever you do, do it well.

Chapter 38: Strength & Power

I toured deep into a federal maximum security prison a couple of years out of graduate school. It was a small group of six or so of us whose research and policy work involved criminal sentencing. The prison was full of dangerous, hardened criminals whose incentive for not crushing my skull with a fire extinguisher was basically a loss of commissary privileges or something. I mean they were already in prison for decades or life, so there's only so much you can do to punish them. Anyway, it was a time I felt at-risk, uneasy, threatened, even a little helpless.

Two of the people in the group were young women. And the inmates basically all lurched and yelled at them like a long line of loud, aggressive pit bulls pulling hard at the ends of their chains. As unnerving as the experience was for me that day, I can only imagine what it was like for those women. On top of the threat of violence I faced, those women faced another very real threat of sexual assault.

In general, men don't think about things like this. They just don't come up very often for most of us. But it's important to understand that women face this all the time in ways small and large. Basically just being out in the world can be a risk to safety – to life – in ways that don't happen that much to men (unless you are a person of color). Sure, in some rough places in the world, men face constant risk, but even in those places, the danger to women is usually greater. And for most of the people reading this book, those neighborhoods, those parts of the world, are places to be avoided, social issues to deal with, plot lines to TV shows and movies. They aren't *our* world.

You can define strength and power all sorts of ways. Here, I use "strength" to mean physical. Men are, in general, larger and stronger than women. There are plenty of strong women and plenty of weak men. That's not the point. In *general,* men are bigger and stronger.

When it comes to power, in general, men are more likely to wield political, economic, and social power. And men have maintained this power through structural and institutional advantages and biases that kept women locked out. At first legally, then by unspoken rules. As much as this has changed, enough is still intact that undeniable imbalances still exist. You can see these just about anywhere you look, and if you point out something that *is* balanced, it's probably an exception.

Men have done so many incredibly awful things to women, and to weaker or disadvantaged groups, that when you have a sense of our world's history, it can be hard not to have a dim view of my gender.

Because of this, throughout my life, the conversation with women I know has always involved trying to pass along an understanding of what men can really be like and sharing thoughts on how best to avoid the damage we inflict. The difference between a lovely man full of empathy and a violent abuser can be hard to spot, especially early on in a relationship. Men are just predatory sometimes. For women, this all adds up to a shitty place to be.

When one of my daughters became a thinking and aware teenager, we were having this conversation about men. She stopped, thought for a second, and said "Daddy, why don't we teach the boys not to rape?" Well, that knocked me back on my heels. Because of course she was right, and that is absolutely the solution. But what I was in effect saying with my discussions of how to protect yourself in a world of men was that I had given up on men. Because for every kind and sweet, caring, and thoughtful man in the world, there are probably two violent, abusive, or dangerous a-holes. And half the time you can't tell them apart until it's too late.

I have been thinking about that conversation for a few years now. It nags at me. As much as I still believe we have to teach girls to protect themselves from the world, we really don't do enough to teach boys not to be dangerous to others.

That's what this chapter is about. Whatever strength and power we have as men, it's about what we do with it and what we don't.

It's not about perpetuating a stereotype that women can't take care of themselves. It's about who we are as men and the things we do that hurt others. It's about changing our own behaviors and about calling them out in others. It's about being an ally and not silently standing by with our hands in our pockets, excuses at the ready.

Or do you want to end up in that weird dystopian future where men are banished to the wastelands because we are just not worth the trouble?

As a running coach and volunteer who is around children, I have to participate in mandatory training every year. The information is mostly about being able to identify signs of child sex abuse, knowing when and how to report suspicious behaviors, and a reminder that one-on-one time with minors is to be avoided.

All good advice in our world, but I bring it up here because of the stats they show each time I go through it. One of them is that 96% of all child sex abuse is committed by men. And another is that 90% of the abusers are known to the child or the family (not strangers). It is a painful reminder that we, as men, are almost all of the problem.

In that dystopian future, policymakers could rationally say that no men can be around children, that the risk is just too high. And they'd be right, in a way. But at what cost to the children and to all the men who are not child abusers? At what cost to everyone else? This is the ugly choice that should make every man care about policing themselves – and about policing others.

Because if we don't, well, wherever that ends up, it won't be good.

What can you do? I look at it two ways. One is rooted in the story of Camelot and King Arthur: Be a knight. Use strength and power to help others. Never for the wrong reasons. It's a simple code to understand, and though fictional, it is a clear guide star on how to live.

The other way comes from Christian faith. Paraphrased poorly by me, it says how you treat the least among us is how you are treating Jesus.

There are surely other ways to look at this, from other faiths, other cultures, but take your pick: Be a knight, be a warrior, or be a man of faith, but be a man who stands up for what's right. Be a man who doesn't bully, who doesn't hurt, who says "No" when someone else does it.

It doesn't matter who the target is, or what gender, race, religion they follow, or who they love.

In the end, it doesn't matter what motivates you to check yourself and to stand up to others, to use your strength and power for good; it doesn't matter how you get there. Just get there.

Chapter 39: Words Matter

"Hey guys. What are you guys doing tonight?" We use "guys" without thought for groups of men, and groups of men and women. And if you ask the guys, they would probably tell you it doesn't mean anything.

But if we addressed a mixed group as "ladies," it *would* matter. Flipping it around makes it clear that words creep into usage that carry meanings, subtle or not. The group who sees those words as harmless is usually the dominant group in that context. In the U.S., that's typically male and White.

We've evolved enough that many of the harmful words involving race have been largely banished. And in recent years, words such as "retarded" are thankfully headed that way too. But retarded is a good example. People use it to describe something they think is dumb without malice or intent to insult disabled people. And because those of us using it are typically not dealing with a mental disability, *we* don't think it means anything. Again, the dominant "groupthink."

And if reading this far has made you uncomfortable, well, don't be a pussy. Man up. Grow a pair. Or are you going to cry like a girl? Are you strong, decisive, powerful? You must have big cojones. Are you daring? Oh you're ballsy.

We make strength masculine. We feminize weakness. It's really that simple. Some of it is underpinned by the fact that men, in general, are bigger and stronger than women. And that perhaps testosterone leads to more of those "manly" behaviors we value in our culture (and lots of harmful ones too, see Chapter 38, Strength & Power).

What can you do? Start with some baby steps. Change "pussy" to "baby." It takes a little practice, but it works. Change "cry like a girl" to "cry like a baby" (they cry a *lot*). And really, just ditch all the testicle references. Be creative. Challenge yourself to come up with meaningful notions of strength that aren't only masculine. He's as tough as a woman in the delivery room. Something. You'll get another benefit of breaking away from clichés, which will make whatever you say and write more interesting.

Here's an easy one: Ditch the qualifiers. You look great for your age. You're strong for a woman. They make your compliments, at best, backhanded. This is a fantastic place to Stop at the First Sentence. We dug into this more broadly in Chapter 25, Know When to Hush. But here, use a variation, and end the thought where it should. You look great. You're strong.

I kept thinking about compliments when I was working on this, and they kept pairing with the word "creepy" in my head. Men do this a lot. And they always think they are saying something nice.

The words matter a lot. "You look great in that dress" means "That dress highlights your body nicely. Also, I am looking at your body and I like it." How about "That's a great dress!"? Different, right? So many "nice" things men say fall into two categories of subtext: I like your body and want it, or the compliment I just gave you has the phrase "…for a girl" tacked onto the end, whether said or not. This is what we have to watch for and stop.

Variations of this are applied to people of color, especially those from other countries or cultures. Watch the compliments that sound like or imply someone did well but only because your White people expectations of them were low. It's like the "…for a girl" qualifier tacked on the end, but "…for a [anything else]."

Words matter. People don't know what you're thinking. They don't know what's in your heart. They know what you say and what you do. You can say "I'm not like that," all you want, but if you don't care enough to show it with your words, then you are telling people something else.

The old saying "sticks and stones will break my bones, but names will never hurt me," was a way to help deal with hurtful things people said. But it does not mean the words didn't hurt. It does not mean you are free to say whatever you want. It just was pointing out that it wouldn't physically harm you. They do hurt. Words matter. Really, this is just being a bully. And why would you want to be that person?

Now let's talk about humor. It's such a wonderful thing, but it is abused by the asses among us. It has a time and a place, but if your humor is cutting down someone else, it's only funny to you. It's just mean. If it's funny at someone else's expense, it's just mean.

People get fired for saying hurtful things. So just stay on the side of nice with your humor. Showing someone how clever you are, how observant of the odd little details in our lives you are, is just not worth it. It's not worth hurting people to show off this way, and at the very least, it's not worth your job.

And even if it's not mean, embarrassing, or ridiculing, there are plenty of times what's funny at a bar is not funny in the office. Context is key, and so is time and place. And no matter where you are, jokes about race, religion, gender, sexuality, ethnicity (to name some big ones) are not funny. They are mean. They hurt. The only people who can joke about any particular group are members of that group. Not you from the outside. No matter how clever you think it is.

And here's a pro tip: If you felt the need to say "Just Kidding," it wasn't funny; it was mean.

While we're here, let's divert for a bit into attacking the message, not the messenger. It might seem obvious, but given our current political climate, I don't think it is. See Chapter 67, Attack the Message.

And make sure to tie this in with how you approach communicating with others (see Chapter 7, Communication). Because you can have all the best intent and a good soul, and still screw it up if you don't get the words right. The good news here is that these mistakes can be avoided most of the time just by being aware and paying attention to your word choices.

Words show what we value – and what we don't. They show people who you are, so choose them carefully, choose them with respect, choose them with kindness.

Chapter 40: Dude Bros & Empty Girls

There's a guy you know. He wears baggy shorts and a t-shirt, his hat's on backward. He plays violent video games, loves videos of people getting hurt doing stupid stuff. He basically stopped maturing when he hit 14. Dude Bro.

There's a girl you know. She spends all her time on her clothes, her looks, and her social media image. She basically stopped growing when she hit 16. Say hi to Empty Girl.

If we're lucky, they found each other so we don't have to deal with them.

These are broad stereotypes for sure, and you probably know lots of variations of these two. Variations that change based on geography or culture or ethnicity, whatever. It could be sports, or celebrity culture, or anything at all. It could be a Dude Girl or Empty Bro, it doesn't matter, you know who they are.

And it's important to hear this part: It doesn't mean you can't enjoy pastimes that are simple and fun. Please don't hear that. What we're talking about here is when a few shallow things are *all* there is.

Why do these people matter? Well, for starters, there are a *lot* of them in the world. They impact everything from what dominates in pop culture to the literal and figurative "guard rails" we put up pretty much everywhere to keep them alive – guard rails that annoy the rest of us.

They also make your personal and professional life harder and more frustrating. They don't pay attention, they don't learn, and they don't care about most things. The things that are interesting to them are mostly shallow and silly to the rest of us.

There's just not that much there. Empty Girls and Dude Bros.

What can you do? Enjoy sharing time with them if it's something that works for you, but insulate yourself. Keep them at the edges of your life. Don't let them in all the way. But be nice about it; they don't know any better. Don't try to change them or "fix" it. And if they are in your family or your workplace, and so you have to interact at least sometimes, then remind yourself who they are, don't expect more, and budget extra time and patience to get through anything with them.

And if you are reading this and see a little of yourself, what can you do? Well, for starters, let's not kid ourselves here. If you are one of them, you're not reading this book, because, well, it's a book. But just to humor me and pretend there's hope for our future, I'll throw out a couple of suggestions:

The most important one is that no matter who you are, or what you care about (or don't care about in this case), try to consider others, how they feel, and what's important to them. Don't be an ass. Basically, try to be a Decent Human Being.

This is especially true if your version of Dude Bro includes aspirations to Master of the Universe status. That's where you become something like the cliché trader on Wall Street who cares only about $1,000 bottles of vodka and how many expensive watches he has. We will always have these people among us, so all we can ask is that they try to dial back just how much of a raging jackass they are, and try to keep it to themselves and their small group of like-minded souls who will appreciate them for who and what they are.

Chapter 41: Mansplaining

I was wrestling with whether women can be mansplainers (they can), and mentioned this internal debate out loud. I was promptly mansplained to by a man that I was defining mansplaining incorrectly. This made me wonder briefly whether the moment would rip a hole in the fabric of the universe.

It made me realize that if you don't think you've experienced mansplaining, then you probably aren't paying attention, are not sure what it is, or are the one doing it all the time. Also, you're probably a man.

What is mansplaining? That was a weird question for me. Not only how to define it, but also how to do it without being a mansplainer about it. This would be another time when the irony would not be delicious.

One of the better explanations I saw read like a flow chart. First, did a woman *ask* you to explain? If so, you're good to go. If not, see No. 2.

Second, do you have more relevant experience on the topic? If you answer yes, then you *might* be OK. But you're still on shaky ground if she did not ask.

Third, are you *assuming* the answer to question No. 2? Sometimes men are a bit full of ourselves in a way that creates a "yes" to question No. 2 when it's not really not quite so.

Women do it too, though I am pretty sure it's a tiny percentage compared with men. But when men do it, the impact is greater because of all the baggage we bring. Not least of which are common biases of assuming women and people of color have less knowledge or understanding of whatever topic is at hand.

Not even a week after having mansplaining mansplained to me, I was having a discussion in a running group about an elite-level female runner who had written a great piece on her decision to stop competing at the championship level and focus on the next phase of her life. The mansplainer in the group promptly explained why she was doing it and what it meant. Then he explained to all of us how it wasn't relevant because she was a national elite runner while we were local hobby-joggers. So a man, who isn't an elite athlete, was explaining the relevance and motivations of a woman he didn't know, and who *was* an elite athlete.

For me, this brings up another variation of the classic mansplainer I want to weave in here too: The Expert Commenter. The Keen Observer. The Knower of All Things. These titles are all self-appointed, of course. They assume they know why something is, that they know the background, the motivation, of whoever said whatever they are commenting about.

No matter the type of behavior here, the dominant flavor tastes of condescension. You come across as patronizing, and even if you weren't going to be mansplaining, just explaining, well, you are now.

Whether you think you do it or not, here are two tips that might help you avoid it: Don't launch into an explanation that isn't sought. And don't assume your audience knows less than you do.

Another strategy I find useful is to ask questions. I do that a lot, mostly to protect my listeners from hearing *way* more than they care to about some topic I find interesting. Asking questions helps me find out what they already know and their level of interest in the topic.

This strategy of asking questions is useful along many facets of leadership, working in groups, and in relationships in general. Getting into the habit will be a big plus. And it will help you avoid being a mansplainer. This is a good thing, for everyone.

But if you're on the receiving end of it, how can you deal with it?

This question came after a friend read a draft of this chapter. She asked whether I would tackle how to deal with mansplaining when it happens to you. My first thought was "Sure, I'm going to mansplain how to manage mansplainers. That's going to go well." Then I thought, "Well, she *asked* for my input, so maybe I'm in OK territory."

Dealing with mansplainers can be done in all sorts of ways. I don't think there's a single strategy. It depends on your personality and tolerance for conflict, as well as the subtleties of the relationship and the politics of the environment.

If you are comfortable with a direct approach that has a little bite, try laughing at him. Or maybe patting his little head and saying, "That's so cute," or something.

If you can get away with a little snark, try something like "Please, do tell all of us exactly how to do our jobs. We didn't know you are an expert in all of these areas." Or "Oh, I didn't know it was time to tell each other how to do our jobs. Is it my turn now?"

Another important variable is how quick your style is. I have a good friend who is smart and great at her job, but she's a processor, so she takes a little time to run something through her head and end up somewhere. For her, it takes the snappy retort off the table as an option. It's just not how she works. So, she needs a different strategy. And so would the people who don't do conflict and confrontation well.

For them, if you are in the right place and time to use a little sarcasm, think through how to address the behavior the next time it happens. My processor friend has a guy on the team who goes on and on about himself and how awesome he is. I suggested she actually put him on the next meeting agenda with something like: "9-9:15, Cam talks about Cam. 9:15-9:30, Cam tells everyone how to do their jobs." This can be funny, and sometimes disarming, and lead to healthy conversations.

It can also go very wrong. Snark and confrontation have risks you have to assess for your environment. You need to consider the time and place, the culture and the audience, your delivery, and the relative statuses of the people involved. I wouldn't push this one if it's not a natural fit for you or in the right environment to do it.

When it happens to me, it's not so much mansplaining as it is people underestimating me, so they tell me lots of things I already know. Or at least that's how it feels. Some of it is innocent enough. They really don't know what you know. Lots of times though, it can make you bristle because of the *assumption* that you don't know anything. This probably happens to a lot of people, though my sense is it happens to women far more often simply because they are women. Bonus layer of annoyance.

Being underestimated has its uses though. It can be an advantage in competitive and adversarial situations. Not so much in situations that involve what your boss or your team thinks of you, however. You have to be the judge of whether you can turn the irritating behavior into something useful, or whether you need to knock it down.

This assessment is important because one of the ways to deal with mansplaining is to just ignore it. You didn't ask for the opinion, so brush it off. But I don't suggest ignoring in contexts where doing that might hurt you, only the ones where it doesn't matter and where he's just not worth the trouble.

When it *is* worth addressing, and sarcasm and snark don't work for you or in your environment, then a calmer, less-risky approach is to think through how you want to address it, and then do it privately. You might not get anywhere. You might just get a defensive mansplain about why you're wrong to accuse him of mansplaining. But you did the right thing and you tried.

Try asking questions to make sure the intent matches what you heard; confirm the mansplaining. Then ask questions to see whether you can get him to see what happened and how it comes across. Worth a shot, because if he happens to be open to learning and growing, your life will be better, and you might spare a bunch of other people from his behavior too.

If all else fails, you don't have to get him to see that it's mansplaining. You can still try to make your life better even if he won't see what he's doing.

Try explaining how you see the behavior or how it made you feel. Then articulate the specific things that need to change in how he interacts with you. Make sure to let him know that you will help make this work by pointing it out each time going forward – not to be a jerk, but to reinforce the new behavior until it sticks.

If it's your boss carrying on, try something like this: "I appreciate the detail on this topic, but it's my job to know this, and so I think we can make better use of both of our times if we don't rehash what we both already know." Bosses are tricky beasts, so you have to gauge how direct you can be with this. You may need to tone these words down even more than my example, or not say them at all. You know your boss; I don't. Tread carefully here.

Whether it's working on yourself or pushing back on others, we need to turn mansplaining into something for the history books. It might not be the most pressing problem, or even the most irritating thing, but it feels to me like one we can change with the smallest of effort and just about zero cost.

Chapter 42: Don't Be Gross

Have you ever walked into a friend's dorm or apartment and felt like you needed a shower after you left just from being in the room?

When I was a freshman in college, my first roommate smelled bad and his closet smelled worse. Turns out he had no idea how to do laundry (and YouTube didn't exist yet to help him figure it out), so he just kept wearing the same clothes over and over.

It doesn't matter whether you have a big place or a bunch of nice things. It doesn't matter whether you're a person who cares about having a big place or a bunch of nice things. The one thing that signals so much about who you are is whether your home, your life, is just gross.

Where you live can be small, modest, barely furnished, or badly furnished. This can – and should – be different for everyone depending on where you are in life and what you care about. But if it's clean and mostly neat, that makes all the difference in the world. And for the few who will judge because you have to or want to live modestly, well, that's a great indicator that you don't want them in your life anyway.

Going from your parents' place to being on your own for the first time requires some growth that doesn't come easily or automatically for a lot of people. Some people got a lot of practice at home because they had to or wanted to help out around the house. So they might already know how to cook, to clean, to do their own laundry.

But for many of you, these are skills that come over time and out of necessity because you don't want to starve or wear dirty clothes.

There are two big points here: how you manage You and how you affect others.

Let's start with you. Learning to care for and feed yourself. This means buying groceries, cooking, laundry, and cleaning. It means all sorts of basic adulting like paying bills, getting your taxes done, scheduling appointments, and getting insurance. It means taking care of the things that matter just enough so that you are OK.

I know this can sound boring, lame, and like a big time-suck, and I can't help you with the boring and lame. Some of it kind of is. It's just the price of entry to adulthood. For the time-suck, though, you can learn to be efficient and minimal, covering the bases just enough to get by in a decent way.

Ask someone who already has it together. Ask your parents. Google it. Watch a YouTube video. I swear there's a video for anything, no matter how mundane or trivial.

Just keep your home, your car, and your desk clean enough that you look like a grown-up. And, yes, your home includes the bathroom.

When it comes to cooking, figure it out just enough to stay alive. You might be the sort who prefers to eat out or get take-away most of the time. And if that's how you want to spend your money, and you can do it in a way that's healthy enough to keep you from falling apart, have at it. But even then, being able to manage in a pinch is important.

If you take care of these things, you will cover most of the second focus: how you affect others. No one wants to be in your home, especially your bathroom, if it's disgusting. No one.

At the office, no one appreciates that moldy mess you left in the fridge because you don't care. They don't much like that pig-pen you call a desk either. If you have a car, try not to let it be a trash can or a place where the surfaces haven't been cleaned since you started driving it.

For the times when you are sharing space, having a handle on basic adulting makes you so much easier to live with. And if you make the effort to do your part – like covering your share of the bills, cooking, shopping, and cleaning

– it makes a huge difference in the lives of those around you.

If you think about it, a big chunk of our lives will involve sharing space in some way. We share space in the workplace, we have roommates, and eventually we have partners or spouses.

For pretty much all of these tasks, well, except maybe for keeping yourself clean, it's an option to outsource the work, to get help. When your income exceeds basic living expense levels, those are choices you can make about what's most important to you to do with your time and money. My argument is to do something.

Caring enough to keep You and your world clean, managing basic adulting tasks, and showing the world you care just enough that you don't inflict any of those gross things on them will jump-start you toward being a successful adult human.

Chapter 43: When No One Is Looking

I find money in the street sometimes. You log enough running miles early in the morning maybe the odds are higher? Anyway, when I find it, there's no way to return it to its rightful owner. What I usually do is put it all in the next tip jar I see. This makes me happy to do a small thing, but it also would have been reasonable to keep it.

Now let's change it to a wallet, with ID in it. Now I know who it belongs to, and even though it might be a pain sometimes, I go through the trouble to get it back to its human. There are two reasons for this: It's the right thing to do, and it's what I hope someone would do if they found my wallet.

What you do when no one is looking may be different than the things you do – or don't – because you might get in trouble or be thought less of in a group that's important to you. You might not spend much time thinking about these concepts, but honor, ethics, morality, and integrity are things that make up the very core of who you are. Your actions show you, and everyone else, who you really are. They define your character.

If you damage this character through your actions, it can be hard to repair, especially in the eyes of others. In some ways, the values that you hold dear are all you really have in life.

Do you think you are a good person? If so, why do you think that? Are you consistent with your own values, even when that harms you? Do you follow society's rules, regulations, and laws because that's the price of living in a society? Or do you do that unless they are inconvenient or ones you disagree with?

What this gets at is whether you actually live the way you believe, whether there are consequences or not, whether you'll get any credit or not. Or are your values there only when it's convenient, when it makes you look good? Are your ethics situational?

In society, we give up some rights, like to do whatever we want, in return for the benefits that come with it. That means you give up your right to punish, to be judge, jury, and executioner, for example, or to take whatever you can. And you have to follow the laws and rules of society, even when you don't like them or they are a hassle.

This is often called the "social contract." The way Thomas Hobbes described it in "Leviathan" has always been my favorite. Absent society, we live in a state of nature. There are only two things that matter when we live in the wild, and he termed those "force" and "fraud." These "virtues," as he called them, make sense when you think about an environment with no rules, where nothing is unjust. You do what you want, when you want, and how you want. Whatever you are strong enough or clever enough to take, you can have. There is no morality any more than a lion considers the fate of an antelope.

Hobbes termed life in the state of nature "solitary, poor, nasty, brutish, and short." That pretty much says it all, and it's the big motivation as to *why* we enter into a social contract to live in societies.

It can be easy to rationalize behavior that is not OK, but which benefits us, especially when no one is looking, when you won't get caught. Here are a few clues that you might be doing that. For starters, "everyone does it" is not a hall pass for you. And of course, two wrongs don't make it right. That's an old one, but a good one. And there's a big bucket of "that law/rule/requirement is stupid." Also rationalizing; your opinion of the requirement does not invalidate it.

Let's round out with a favorite of mine: the large organization that either won't miss whatever you are taking or deserves to be cheated. A decent person would remind you that you don't really know whether the loss would hurt that organization, and even if it wouldn't, that's not your call to punish them that way.

Sometimes you are only cheating yourself. You're not hurting society. But that's still a choice, and still cheating. You might rationalize this one too by telling yourself you're not hurting anyone. We both know that's not the point.

I have a runner friend who always had two watches on. Seemed odd. When we asked her one day, the answer was "oh, that's my mom's fitness tracker. She likes getting the credit for all the extra steps from when I run." There are lots of ways to "cheat the system," no matter what "system" we're talking about. But "cheating" is the key word here. Whether you are cheating yourself or someone else – even if it's some large group, like a corporation or a government – the word "cheating" doesn't go away.

The U.S. Naval Academy has a simple honor code: You don't lie, steal, or cheat. Pretty straightforward, and if they catch you violating it, they kick you out. Serious punishment. But the logic is that if we as a nation are to entrust you with life-and-death decisions, we need to be able to count on you to have honor and integrity, to believe you are a Decent Human Being.

If you take this code of don't lie, steal, or cheat, and add in don't hurt people, then you've got a pretty solid foundation to live by. There is much you can add beyond this for your own personal code, matters of faith and conscience that mean something to you. But it all comes down to what you do when no one is looking.

PART IV: It's Not About You

So much of being a Decent Human Being comes from having the perspective, and the awareness, of when It's Not About You. This carries through to leadership, management, relationships, parenting, pretty much everything.

The biggest issues in our workplaces, and in society, get complicated quickly and can overwhelm us if we let them. They are, after all, big and complex.

Gender, sexuality, race, and culture – and all the ways just these four intersect and interact – test our perspectives immensely, create a ton of conflict, and are the subjects of countless books.

In Part IV we will try to distill some of this big stuff down to ideas and guidance useful in our Human Training.

Chapter 44: Judging the Book

"Don't judge a book by its cover," is a wonderful saying that applies, obviously, to books, but also to people and really, to almost anything. A classic variation from Martin Luther King, Jr., says to judge people on the content of their character, not the color of their skin.

But making judgments about people and situations is hardwired into us as a survival mechanism. We need to decide, often in an instant, whether that other human is a predator, an ally, a mate, or background noise. We have to decide whether to run, to fight, to explore a person further, or to ignore them. Mistakes can equal death.

If you are out in the world and see a rabbit or a duck, it will probably scatter pretty quickly if you get too close. These critters instinctively fear the large two-legged beasts. But there's a lake in the heart of my city that tons of people run around all the time. There are lots of ducks and rabbits, and typically, they barely move as we run by. They've learned that we are harmless – and sometimes we have food. Sure, some fool could stomp one on his way to becoming a serial killer, but since these animals are generally left alone, they don't care about us running by.

I was running in the Florida woods one day and came across a herd of hogs. Since they were all across the path, I just sort of barreled through figuring, "Hey, these are just pigs" and that they would scatter. They did. But I was informed later by smarter people that these were *wild* hogs, and there was very likely a big boar in charge who could have felt that I was threatening his herd and proceeded to gore my insides until they were outsides. My ignorance could have been expensive. My snap judgment was wrong.

Trying to justify snap judgments based on appearance is in direct conflict with how this behavior manifests as an all-too-common and generally lousy sort of bias.

How do we resolve this conflict? I look to two ideas for framing that might help.

The first is the Cost of Being Wrong. I use this a lot in my work and in this book. If someone asks you for change to feed a parking meter because they don't have any coins, the cost of being wrong for believing them is that you got hustled out of a dollar. If they want you to invest your life savings into some great thing they have going, then the cost of being wrong is much larger. It's the same with things that affect your personal safety, as one big example.

It doesn't matter who you are inside, if you look and dress and act like a dangerous person, that's how we will react to you. White, Black, Hispanic, or anything else, it doesn't matter. It's better to be wrong, to hurt someone's feelings, than it is to be dead.

I believe that in broad terms, but after I wrote the first draft, a friend pointed out that people can have widely different definitions of "dangerous," especially when race is involved. So a Black guy in jeans and a t-shirt looks like a regular human to me, but to some people, that's a dangerous thug. The challenge with defining "dangerous" is we start to layer in these legacies of racism. This makes my argument to use the cost of being wrong as your key in whether you have time to explore further before you make a snap judgment so much harder to articulate. Because what I mean by "dangerous" has a nuance that is "make the snap judgment if the outcome could be death, but don't be a racist about it." But me adding this important condition isn't going to help. The person making the judgment would say they are not racist.

Where I end up is that we still need to make the judgments that will protect us, but we also need to work together to remove the racist baggage that causes some of us to do this without justification. They are two different issues.

Making snap judgments is built into us. And because it's how we survive life-and-death things (mostly anyway), it doesn't make sense to try to totally change it or ignore it. That's asking too much, and probably not wise. What *does* make sense is to know it's there and build our awareness of when we do it. Then we can work on *not* doing it when we shouldn't.

For the times you make those quick assessments, try to hold them lightly, find a way to confirm, and be ready to adjust completely. I visualize holding ideas lightly between my fingers until I have a good reason, good data, to hold them tighter.

Similarly, tuning your approach based on the audience is smart, but doing it based on assumptions is not. For example, I dial back newer cultural references around an older audience, and I dial back the older references in front of younger audiences. It doesn't mean some people wouldn't have caught the references even with a generational mismatch. It *does* mean making some assumptions that will help you communicate as effectively as you can, assumptions that if wrong, won't harm anyone in the process.

That gets into the second idea I'd recommend you consider (after the Cost of Being Wrong): the *type* of judgments we are making, and the *reasons* we are making them (we *can* change these).

Think about all the times and places we judge people based on appearances: how people dress, what they drive, what they look like, the color of their skin, their gender, how they speak, any disabilities they might have, what they do for a living, their religion – or lack of it. These are the sorts of things that we need to stop and think about first before we speak, before we act.

It really is the simplest of strategies: Don't assume anything about anyone until you get to know them. When we make assumptions about what a woman wants or doesn't, can or can't do, based on her gender, we are failing at being a Decent Human Being. The same with assumptions we make about someone based on their race or anything else. If you look back through the list of examples in the previous paragraph, I suspect you can come up with at least one assumption people might make about any of those attributes.

Be aware of the tendency to make assumptions, and then train yourself to stop doing that outside of survival situations, and to take the extra moment to think and ask questions before you jump to a conclusion. This is how we all do better together.

While we work to make society better at this, it's worth thinking about how people are judging you and why. Then consider whether you want to do anything about it. Consider your behaviors and your choices – the things you can do something about – and know you are being judged. What you say, do, wear, drive, tattoo, pierce, the list goes on. Be willing to accept the consequences, change your behaviors, or fight for acceptance of them.

Chapter 45: My Group Is Better

Groups can be fun. Groups are comforting and comfortable. They are often harmless.

The reality is that your group is probably not all that different from the next group.

In the part of Florida where I am currently trapped, there is a huge number of "Gator" fans. They love the University of Florida and its SEC football team. Lots of these fans didn't even *go* to the school. If you are farther south in the state, maybe you are a Miami fan, farther north in the state, maybe Florida State. Whatever.

All over the country you see it repeat with big state schools and their football or other popular sports teams. And really, setting aside the outright snobbery of the SEC fans, most of the schools and their sports teams are about the same. Sure, there are regional differences, and differences in which sports are dominant, and sometimes even which sorts of academic programs the schools are known for. But in the end, they are big state schools with their groups. All of these differences are small and ultimately, mostly without real meaning.

When my daughter told us about her acceptance into Florida State University, she was actually distraught. What was going to happen when everyone in the family found out? Would they disown her because it wasn't the University of Florida? She was genuinely worried, and it was absurd.

Why does this example matter? Why do any of the group differences matter? They often don't, really. Until they do. Until the tribal nature of humans takes a dark turn.

The key is knowing that the very inclusive nature of our groups effectively excludes others, others who are often hurt by this in ways small and large.

"Hey! You went to Florida? So did I! You're a Gator fan? Me too! You like to go fishing and hang out at the beach? Me too! You're gonna fit in great here at our company!" Hiring practices like this have existed forever and even recently might still be defended as "looking for a good fit with our company's culture." But what you're really doing is hiring someone who looks and acts like you. Someone comfortable and familiar.

You might end up with a good fit for a buddy, but who knows whether it's a good hire for skills and abilities? It's the same when you hire based on age or appearance. And it's the same when you exclude everyone who doesn't look like you or share similar life experiences. We lose diversity. Our decisions aren't as good as they could be. We lose new ideas – and new perspectives – that "outsiders" bring.

This in-group mindset can quickly turn dangerous when we devalue other groups. Time and again in history, the dark side of tribalism is how it became easier to hurt others on a large scale. They were outsiders; they were not like us. That kind of thinking is the first step down a bad road.

What's the point here? Groups can be fun and harmless when you keep them in perspective. When you keep them out of politics, out of the workplace. My school is better than yours. My sports team is better. Whatever. It's fun. But unimportant.

Reaching outside your group in life and especially in the workplace, is how you truly gain diversity in all the ways, in what people look like, how they think, in the experiences and perspective they bring.

It's fundamentally up to you to reach outside your group and not expect others to force their way in, and not expect them to become like you to gain entry.

Chapter 46: Perspective

"I peed myself a little."

"Really? That's AWESOME!"

"What!?"

"Merit-badge stuff. I'm proud of you!"

"What?"

We had just finished a hard running workout on the track. To my training partner, peeing herself was failure. I mean, peeing yourself generally is, right? But to me, it was inspirational. It showed hard work, determination, and dedication. It showed an ability to push through when things are tough. Serious bad-ass.

Perspective.

Yours is yours and not always everyone else's. Getting used to this and making it a part of your thought process will make a world of difference in how you see the world and how well you interact with it.

For sure, it's more work to see the world through other people's eyes. And, said a different way, you have to work harder *not* to see the world only through your eyes.

Missing other perspectives or getting stuck in your own often will result in missing out on something important or misunderstanding how things really are. It will hold you back in relationships and generally everywhere in life. It can also cause real harm to yourself and others in situations where not really understanding what's going on has more serious consequences.

Speed and focus are a big part of *why* we miss other perspectives. We move so quickly, we don't take the extra few seconds to stop and actually think about the assumptions and decisions we make. We focus on the task at hand and on ourselves most of the time. We focus on what makes sense to us, for us. So we don't even consider how it might be very different for someone else.

Take Trevor. He's a dude. He loves to work out, and all his hobbies are active things. And Trevor leads a company with a few hundred on staff. Naturally, Trevor wants to do some team building, because one of his dude-bro fellow execs at the gym was talking about how awesome it was. This of course involves things like zip lines and rope courses. Because it makes perfect sense to Trevor. People will confront their fears (if they have them) together. They will bond. It'll be great.

What Trevor can't even picture is how a huge chunk of his staff is either terrified at the idea, would rather do almost anything else, and for some, do not feel physically capable. This creates so much angst and anxiety – and is the opposite of team building. But he doesn't see that. His smart HR person tried to tell him, and he brushed her off as the buzz-kill. Trevor.

And I see you smiling smugly, Kaitlynn. You know Trevor, and you see all of that. "I'm not like that." I can almost *hear* you thinking it. You know what? Those sharing circles and vision boards, meeting themes and ice breakers? Good grief, you lose half the room each time, and *you* don't even see it. So wipe off that smile and pay attention. This is about you too.

There are lots of things that drive your perspective. Some of the biggest ones are gender, race, sexuality, education, age, religion, and occupation. Most of these have their own chapters so when you finish this book, I hope you have a better perspective about you, and about lots of things that are not about you.

Sometimes our perspectives and biases are a little harder to see. There's a newsletter I read about the world of old vehicles. An article popped up recently that shifted my perspective – and surprised me when it did. In a nutshell, it said that where you are in life has a big influence on your outlook. You might be critical of that kid with a loud, fast, gas-guzzling machine. You might be saying to yourself, or to anyone trapped around you, that "the kid needs to think about the Earth and his neighbors' peace and get a sensible hybrid, or even better, an all-electric vehicle." I mean, sure, it was fine 20 years ago for *you* to have that crazy car, but times have changed, and we all need to be serious and thoughtful.

The article's point was that *you* have changed along with the world. People at 20 are full of energy, and want to have fun and do stupid, wasteful things. You, at 40, are the one who has outgrown it. That doesn't mean everyone else has, or should. This is an important perspective shift for me as I catch myself shaking my head at the fools with their race-ready vehicles and loud exhausts, or their silly jacked-up trucks with lots of neon underneath.

But there's a difference between making space for others to do fun and stupid things, and those things that affect us all. Like having an overly loud exhaust or speeding through neighborhoods to show off. These are the sorts of things that infringe on the peace of others or are even dangerous to others. Anything short of that though, to each their own, right?

All of the differences, the variations of gender, race, age – any of them – are useful to understand. They can both help you see how others might see you and the world, and they can encourage an inward look that might help you to push past the limiting effects of what you naturally value and believe. This can better help you question what you think and understand how others react.

The not-so-secret secret to all of this? Put yourself in their shoes. An old idea, but that's really all it takes. Take the extra few seconds to think about whatever it is you are planning to do or say in the context of your audience, of the person across the table, of the person next to you on the couch.

If you get stuck trying to do that, read a little. Seek out a little background to help you understand a bit better the things you are not. Things about men, women, people of color, people of other faiths, other sexualities and gender identities, abilities, interests, occupations, ethnicities and cultures, regions and traditions, even age.

Spending that time and pushing the focus away from you and toward everyone else will make you stronger, smarter, and healthier in your relationships and careers. It will make you a Decent Human Being because to do this well, you have to understand what other people see – and care enough to weave that into what you say and do.

Chapter 47: White People

Dear White People:

In the previous chapter, we talked about perspective. This chapter is really about one kind of perspective, but one that has such a profound impact on everything around us that it needs its own stage with a solo spotlight.

And no, not because White people are so darn special.

The "White People" perspective is so widespread, so ingrained, that we don't really see it. White people are the "norm." What we do, what we say, eat, read, watch, believe, what we value. White people. The English language. The norm.

If you're in a charitable mood, you could say it makes sense. For so long, most of the United States was English-speaking and White. The Indigenous population was hidden away in rural and remote areas. The Black population was segregated in areas we ignored. The Hispanic and Asian numbers were small and isolated.

We looked to Western Europe because that's the family tree, the history, the traditions, the religion, the philosophy. It is the source of our culture. The entire rest of the planet was a thing to trade with, take resources from, conquer, or ignore. And that Western history traced back to the Greek and Roman empires, and to the writings of the Christian Bible. So, you know, all of history (in our minds). And it was White, even when it wasn't exactly so. In short, it felt like White people *were* the world, *were* its history.

Then we arrive in the 21st Century. Turns out the rest of the world exists, has something to say, and isn't all White and Christian. Turns out the United States, though still largely White and English-speaking, becomes more multicultural and diverse every year.

But here we are, still using White things as the default, the gold standard, the ideal. It's so pervasive that we don't even think "White people," we think "people." We make assumptions about what's right and wrong, good and bad through our White lens. Slowly but steadily though, the rest of the world chips away at the default and says "Hey, there are lots of other things going on."

The progress is unsteady, often with White society needing to be dragged into new things kicking and screaming like a 5-year-old not getting their way. But it's happening.

This overarching perspective is in some way all about privilege. We hear it all the time – "White privilege" or just "privilege." It's a tough thing to hear for most White people. It's an indictment, a finger-pointing at a reality, so the reaction is defensive. I get that reaction. It's like when someone says you're a jerk or a bad person. For most of us, that would hurt.

I also think the word itself – privilege – gets in the way. It rubs people the wrong way because for almost everyone, we didn't grow up with what we consider privilege. I went to an inexpensive state university, worked all the way through college, and took student loans to make it all happen. I worked hard to build a life, worked hard for everything I have. It doesn't *feel* like privilege.

But when you dig into what privilege means in this context, my story still has advantages that the stories of people of color (and women in some ways) don't. Parents with the experiences and resources to point me the right way, to support me in whatever ways they could. A world that expected me to be in college and do OK. A distinct lack of societal and institutional barriers in my way, especially as a White male. Once you start looking at all the things that go into this idea of "privilege" beyond what comes with the wealth that most of us don't have, the idea becomes clear and the reasoning sound.

In talking about privilege, you hear about "resources." But there is another useful way to look at it: It's about "access." Using the term resources probably sounds like money to most people, and it really is in a lot of ways. But there's so much more beyond money. "Access" starts to get at what being White brings along. And it removes the objection we hear all the time to privilege ("I didn't come from money.") Access is how doors are open when you are White, or at least easier to open. It's about the assumptions society makes about what can and should happen that make it smoother for White people to move along in life.

I also think that because White people and Western European culture have dominated the U.S. for so long, there's a little blow-back happening. Some anti-White, anti-Western sentiments bubble up. Seems understandable. The "classics" in literature are attacked. The legends of history. Lots of it warranted, some maybe not so much.

But accepting the reason behind the frustrations, behind the reactions, might help settle White people down. It will help us get to a place where we are a willing part of the transition into the new world, and stop resisting it in an ultimately futile effort to maintain our legacy status of privilege and dominance.

This means seeing people of color, people with other ideas, people who speak other languages, and have other traditions and values become more common in our collective lives. These new faces and ideas become more common in our movies and TV, in our books and music, in our food and art, in our faith and beliefs.

A small example of probably an almost-limitless supply of examples in the world of White people: I grew up thinking that lots of traditional Asian musical styles were weird, even atonal. This is a classic White people view. My stuff is good; your stuff is not. At some point I came to understand the music wasn't off; my ears were. I wasn't familiar with it; didn't grow up with it, so I didn't hear it like I should have. It requires first an awareness that the thing that is off is *you*, not the unfamiliar thing, and then a willingness, an openness, to learn.

We can be a roadblock that will be torn down or detoured around, or we can help build a better road. Which do you want to do?

Chapter 48: Black People

"So you're going to write about Black people?"

"Yep."

"You realize you're a middle-aged White guy, don't you?"

"Yep."

"Do you think this is a good idea?"

"Oh yeah, I think it's a great idea."

Then I got "The Look." You know The Look. Often delivered by a spouse, partner, good friend, or teacher. Head turns a bit. Eyebrows go up. Lips purse just so. It's a visual version of saying *really?* This one came from a friend I talked with when I was getting ready to write the chapters in this section. She is a highly educated and professional woman of color who has a low tolerance for nonsense. Yep, I got The Look.

First off, and this is really important: I make no attempt to talk about what the world is like for people of color. That would be foolish, and would make my friend right.

What I do want to talk about are a few things that we might be able to use as common reference points – and sprinkle in a few ideas too – so we can work together on some challenging issues in our society.

If you look at the readers this book targets, by one measure you are all largely college graduates (or expect to be). If that's about a third of adults in the U.S., we've already dropped out a lot of people from this conversation. And if Black people are about 13% of the population, you can see quickly that most of the readers of this book probably will be White. So, hey, White people, let's talk.

And to all the people of color reading, my apologies for saying things you already know.

The Black Lives Matter movement, for example, has become a black and white issue, a forced binary choice (See Chapter 59, Nonbinary World). You hear responses such as "all lives matter," or "blue lives matter" because there are plenty of people who want to frame it as an idea where you have to choose.

Of course, it's pretty easy to argue that supporting the idea that Black lives matter doesn't take away at all from caring about the lives of White people – or the lives of law-enforcement officers. These are not competing issues.

What I hear from this movement is simple: Can we please agree that Black lives matter just as much as everyone else's and start acting that way?

When I was a kid we moved from California to New Hampshire, a pretty White place. My perspective at the time went like this (and yes, my brain already worked in the same logic-path way it does now, just with much less data): The people of color I saw often were from news footage of civil rights marches and protests. And since it was black and white footage, that meant it was old. It was history. And since I knew that Martin Luther King, Jr., had done good things and that we had civil rights laws, we must be OK now. Yes, this wasn't very sophisticated, but I was 10.

It's easy to end up in a place like that. To look at the world with a White perspective, often with limited data about what's going on in other places outside our little piece of the world. I've heard White people argue that there's no more racism because we had a Black president. Or that because there are Black doctors, lawyers, judges, and business owners, things are fine.

I've never heard a person of color say that.

And I've had more than one conversation where I hear how Black people often hide what they go through from White people, like they've given up trying to get us to see it and just share the experiences with family or friends who are Black. There's a snarky thread in my head that Black people are also quiet about this to protect delicate White sensibilities. But I'd guess it has more to do with avoiding the conflict that probably comes from upsetting the White people by pointing out problems that are their fault.

How many of us never really think about getting pulled over by police? How many of us never really think about getting followed in a store, or getting profiled based on skin color?

And getting past those common examples, ones that sometimes feel like we've oversimplified things just to help White people "get it," there are countless others. Some subtle, some not so much.

What about being the only person of color in the room or at the conference table? What about looking on a website and not seeing anyone who looks like you? What about looking at positions of power and authority and seeing White faces all the time? For every way we've done better as a society, such as broadening who we see in our TV and movies, or in the ads we see, there are other disparities that as White people we probably don't even notice haven't changed a bit.

The point is that just because we don't see it, doesn't mean it's not there, it doesn't mean it is "fixed."

I run early in the morning, and recently on a weekly outing with a friend, we were running through a large, empty, and mostly dark local college that was near the trail where we started. I saw a police cruiser parked in the dark and thought, here's a couple of White people running through a dark campus, and this police officer isn't going to care at all. And I wondered how it would go if I were a Black man running through there.

We take these simple things for granted, and it can be helpful to the conversation if we learn to stop taking them for granted; to be mindful that while White perspective seems universal to us – the default – it isn't. People of color often experience the world in very different ways.

While I am on the running theme, which unfortunately for you, is probably too often in this book: We were having a discussion within the leadership of our local running club about what we could do in our community to be more actively inclusive. This came to the forefront after reading about a Black runner in another state getting accosted and killed while he was out running because he looked sketchy to a couple of White dudes. And some of the people of color we talked with relayed stories from my own community that were tough to hear. One was about a Black man who will only run in his *own* nice neighborhood if he has his dog or a friend with him, so he looks "safe." I can run just about anywhere I want and not think about it. Another was a woman afraid for her Black teenaged son to run anywhere alone. White parents don't really have to think about that for their sons.

Let's add a couple of other ideas to the mix: When you think about data – and I do, all the time – it's OK to look at race and gender, and all sorts of other ways we are different from each other. This can be interesting and healthy. It can be a way to learn and grow.

The key is *how* you do it and how you talk about it. The NBA, for example, is mostly Black. That's just data. If you tell me there are 15 players on a team and ask me how many are Black, I would guess about 12 of them. Again, that's just data. But if I meet a Black man who is tall, it's not OK to ask him whether he plays basketball. That's not data; that's an assumption driven by a stereotype. This distinction is important.

The fans of hip-hop and rap might be mostly Black, but it's not OK to ask a Black woman whether she likes Kanye's new release. What is OK is to ask her what new music she's been listening to and take it from there. Maybe she's a fan of classical music, or jazz, hell, maybe even Taylor Swift, and thinks Kanye is a doofus. Who knows?

Try looking at it this way: Any person of color you know or meet is not some sort of ambassador of their culture to the White people. You can ask a friend whether they are willing to share how they feel about an issue, but not how an entire culture feels about an issue.

Don't say to the Black guy you just met, "Hey, do you like basketball?" You might as well have started that sentence with "Hey, you're Black, you must like basketball!" Try this: "Hey, you into sports?" That's a fair question for anyone. Whatever the answer, it can start real conversations.

And so much of how White people view Black Americans is really about poverty. Racist legacies and unequal structures in our society created the poverty, but the outcomes can often be viewed by looking at the impacts and drivers of poverty.

Take all the things you might have heard White people say about the Black community, and go look at a poor White rural county, and you'll often see the same problems. Too many men in jail. Too many single-parent families. Drug and alcohol addictions. Low educational attainment. High unemployment, especially among men. You name it. This is not some defect in the Black community; it's the brutality of poverty.

Learning to see other views and other perspectives is how we can start better conversations about where we go from here. What can you do? Stop with the assumptions. Take the time to imagine walking in someone else's shoes. Take the time to learn. The conversations will go better. We will be better.

Chapter 49: Other People

"White, Black, and Mexican."

I used to work with a kind and decent human who, when something ignorant happened, he'd say to me in a fake, exaggerated drawl: "Well, I tell you, to the good ol' boys around here, there's only three races: White, Black, and Mexican."

That's stuck with me for a long time. He was making a point in one sentence that will take me far more to articulate. The "Mexican" part. Where I live, there are lots of people from places like Mexico, Cuba, and Puerto Rico. And often they all get lumped together. Then they get lumped together along with people from India, the Middle East, and everywhere else. White is White. Black is Black, and every other person of color is, in his telling of the story, Mexican. The label itself doesn't matter. And it doesn't matter what it really is, we just think "not White."

After chapters on White people and Black people, it's important to talk about the world of differences we put into "people of color." I called this chapter "Other People" to try to capture the standard view in the U.S., the White-people view: We look at our society as White, Black, and everyone else.

People from, just to name a few, Central and South America, from the Caribbean, from anywhere in Asia, India, and the Middle East, are all the same to many Americans. And though they are all different, they likely share a great many experiences from being someone in the U.S. who isn't White, maybe not Christian.

When we confront issues we face in the U.S., so much of our conflict comes from gender, race, and political outlook. Outside of those, when I think about race – and ethnicity too – I can't help but feel that much of this conflict is really driven by cultural differences.

We started this discussion in Chapter 45 on Groups and pick it up here. We've always been comfortable in our own groups and wary of outsiders. We like the way things are, and are suspicious, sometimes hostile, to new things, to different things. None of this is new, and a lot of this is built-in, so to me, a useful approach is gaining awareness and then working to manage it.

Different cultures are, well, different. Super obvious, right? Those differences make lots of people uneasy. We filter what's new through the lens of our understanding of the world, especially through the lens of how things are in our group.

This causes us to look at the world in skewed ways and to make lots of assumptions about how other people are, and about what they do and why. And it's magnified when those things seem different. Taking the time to learn about others, to think, to hone your awareness, and to put yourself in someone else's shoes will help you scrape away most of these biases.

My daughter's boyfriend has family in India. That doesn't mean I can ask him what he thinks of an Indian restaurant in my town. I have no idea, until I get to know him, how much he's connected to or cares about his heritage. Maybe he doesn't even like Indian food. If he does, then I'd still need to find out how much he knows or cares about it. Plus, India is a big place, and there are regional variations that would be like asking someone from San Francisco to weigh in on a New York pizza.

People do this stuff all the time. We make assumptions based on heritage, culture, and skin color. It's pretty easy to train yourself to stop. Just assume you don't know anything without asking. Take it as a challenge not to assume anything, and another challenge for your own growth to learn by asking, and by asking well.

A good place to start is ditching the "where are you from" question. For most people, in the U.S., the answer will be, "um, the U.S.," and you rightfully will look like a jerk. I suspect just about every American you meet who doesn't fit neatly in the White or Black box has been asked this, probably often.

Next, think about the typical things we get wrong. How often do we assume that anyone of color is Muslim, when the U.S. has lots of people tracing their heritage to places such as India or a variety of Asian countries – people whose faith might just as easily be Catholic, Hindu, something else, or none at all?

How often do we lump everyone from Hispanic or Latino backgrounds into one monolithic group? I saw the thought-provoking idea surface recently that even the term "Hispanic" is more of a White-people contrivance than a real thing. The example the writer used was that a White Cuban, Black Puerto Rican, and Indigenous Guatemalan are all different people with different experiences, but with our typical labels? All Hispanic.

In our history, this "otherness" often comes with a language conflict. Because most people speak English in the U.S., it makes sense to me that we'd want new arrivals to learn enough to get by. And it makes sense to me that we'd help that process and make the transition easier with certain things printed in more than one language, especially Spanish given the size of that demographic compared with all the others.

But when we get past that thought, we often see hostility or downright anger when people don't speak English well or at all. For those who feel that hostility, part of it stems from a natural preference for our own group and its characteristics. Part of it stems from an aversion to things that are perceived as different. It comes out too often not as an instinct to overcome or manage, but an ugliness, even violence, that no one should have to endure. And that no one should be showing their children.

And when it comes to displays of culture, the easiest thing to do is leave alone anything that isn't part of your culture. I think most people understand why you don't wear a Jewish yarmulke (the skullcap) if you're not Jewish. Same with the Bindi ("dot" on the forehead) unless it's part of your culture, which is generally Hindu, or in modern times, at least culturally Indian.

White people seem to have generally let go of the feathers of Indigenous peoples and claims of being a warrior, brave, or chief. But cultural appropriation of this kind takes longer to work through in society because lots of people think they aren't doing anything disrespectful, or even may think they are honoring the culture with the use. After all, we are using the feathers to show strength and courage, right? Right. But when people from the culture involved are interviewed, it's almost always a problem for them. We just don't seem to ask before we do it. And we say, from our White perspective, something like: "I don't see why this is a problem." That, in a nutshell, *is* the problem.

As we become more diverse, more global, we keep bumping up against new ways to be insensitive, often by people who mean no ill intent at all. Every time I see an actor put his hands together in a non-contact greeting, or when a yoga instructor does it and adds a "namaste" to it, I cringe a little. It's one of those ways we've taken something and stripped it of context and repurposed it for us. We didn't dig deep enough to learn whether it was OK.

Beyond this problem of cultural appropriation, there are things we do that aren't quite right. Have you ever watched a White person try to adopt the speaking style of someone who is different? Usually it's of someone who is Black or Hispanic. It's always cringey and weird.

Like perspective and groups, this is another area that just requires a little thought, a little learning, an open mind, and building a habit of putting yourself in someone else's shoes.

Chapter 50: The Gender Spectrum

The idea of a very definite binary man and woman has been with us forever. You had to fit in your box and it didn't go well most of the time if you didn't. You either hid how you didn't fit and were miserable, or you were open about it, and people around you made you miserable.

How many times have you read in a book or seen in a movie this idea: the girl looking out the window at the boys playing or training? Learning to shoot a bow, fight, build things, ride a horse, whatever. And she's stuck inside learning to cook, sew, make conversation, prepare to be a wife, and so on. And it's not for her at all, but she's stuck. Or maybe it's tolerated that she's a "tomboy" until it's time to become a woman and follow that path and fit in that mold.

And how many times have you seen the reverse of that scene? The boy who is supposed to learn, like, and be good at all the "manly" wonderful things is terrible at them, doesn't like them at all, and is ridiculed and abused by his peers, and often by his own father too.

I find it useful to think of gender as a spectrum: from highly masculine (maybe even toxically so) on one end, to extremely feminine on the other end. And we all fall somewhere along this spectrum.

From a data perspective, this would correlate neatly and strongly with their sex. All that means though is that men would cluster toward the masculine and women toward the feminine. But how far along you are on the spectrum is individual, and whether you are even on the end of the spectrum consistent with your biology is individual.

I would think the testosterone in males and estrogen in females drives some of this in broad strokes of the brush. But that leaves room for lots of variance in how much of either of those hormones is natural in you – and what you do with it.

What we've done, though, is force all the boys into one stereotype and all the girls into another. And for so many children, and later as adults, it just doesn't fit.

This has one of the easiest solutions: Let everyone be whatever they are.

The trouble with that easy thing is it requires all of us to change some behaviors we've been doing forever. We make assumptions about who you are – and what you like and don't like – based on your gender. We make assumptions about what you can and can't do based on your gender. These are partly evolutionary shortcuts we use to make snap decisions. And they are trained into us through society and through the roles we see around us.

One tangent that's darkly comic to me: Some of the negative things are shifting positively, such as objectifying women less. But I've noticed another trend at the same time: We objectify men more. Look at what beauty and fitness standards are for men compared with just a generation ago. Now, men have to be ripped and pretty. Looks like we're going to meet in the middle – for now anyway – instead of fixing it for women all the way. So it's fair in a weird way, but still wrong. But sometimes I wonder if there's some poetic justice in men being judged this way: By how youthful, attractive and lean they are?

Anyway, we've made so much progress even since my kids were born, but only a man (mostly anyway) would tell you that we've made enough, or that it's all OK now.

It's hard to unlearn what we've learned. It's hard to ignore our evolutionary instincts. But we can work on discarding the outdated ones that are no longer useful. It's just a bit more work and takes a bit more time. The payoff for you and for all of us will be worth it.

First, stop assuming anything about anyone based on what you perceive as their gender. Ask, listen, and learn. That's how you find out who someone is and what they like. Second, commit to being part of the solution if you start a family. Stop fostering those stereotypes and shortcuts. Let your boys play with dolls. Let your girls go screaming through the mud on a mountain bike. Whatever it is, doesn't matter; encourage exploration and growth. Let them call themselves whatever they want. Let them go where they go on that journey.

Chapter 51: The Only Sexuality…

…that you get to have an opinion about is your own.

I wanted to end this chapter right there. That one thought says it all. And it would have been cool to have a one-sentence chapter. Alas, it's not enough. We need to talk it through.

Tradition and upbringing may drive what you want, what you think is right. But it shouldn't dictate what others should do.

We like tradition; we like consistency. It's comfortable. It's easy to manage and easy to predict. It's like always swimming in the same waters, especially calm ones.

But change happens. Change is ongoing. It always has been. We are different from our parents – and from those long before them too.

When you look back through history, nearly every generation believed or did something that we wouldn't do now. We evolve; we grow. Getting stuck on this particular issue isn't helping.

I get that it's a big one for a lot of people. Whatever you feel, that becomes natural and normal to you. It's a given, the standard, the norm. It becomes the right thing to you. The only thing. This might make anything else seem strange and wrong to you. This is hard to overcome.

Then we layer in faith – one of the most powerful and important things in our society – and finding the common ground gets that much harder.

Let's try this view: Your faith may dictate what you believe, but not what others should.

Government and social policy should accommodate all faiths – and those without it – not just *your* faith's dictates. The whole point of our heritage, of this grand American experiment, is to be free to worship without the government telling you what you must or must not believe. It's important to remember that when you are inclined to have the government force your beliefs on everyone else.

When we look at social and government policies outside of those driven by faith, those driven more by tradition and history, that changes the view a little. Because in our democracy, what's OK is whatever the majority (sometimes a super-majority) says is OK. I don't mean that to sound flippant, but it's how this works. If we decided that no one could have dogs, and we enshrined that in our laws, through legal means, well, it's legal.

We often lose sight of that in these debates. We get to choose what we put into law, and the bigger stuff we put in our Constitution. Religion, philosophy, morality, ethics, all of it, these come into play, but ultimately, what's right and wrong is whatever we say it is.

This means that it's up to everyone to be heard. To add your voice to the side that believes what's important to you.

But while we're here, let's try another view: Why does who someone loves matter to you at all? How does it affect you personally?

If it's because of your faith, then remember your belief only applies to those who share your faith. You can seek to convert others to your beliefs if spreading the word is part of your faith. You can advocate for society to align with your beliefs, because that's democracy.

If it's just because you don't like change or something that's different, that's on you to get over.

But I suspect in both scenarios, if you try to dictate who people love, you will end up on an ugly side of history when those who come later look back on us.

Chapter 52: About Men

Men are big dogs that talk.

I heard that from a comedian once, and it stayed with me. For lots of men, it's not too far off. We are simple things who like to eat, sleep, play, and be petted.

Or, men are just large 5-year-olds.

Feed us, dress us, take care of our needs, clean up after us, put all of our terrible art on the fridge, and tell us how amazing we are all the time. Make us the nonstop center of your attention.

I've actually suggested both of those to frustrated female friends as a way to understand us – and manage us. And I say those things only a little in jest.

I can make fun of men because I am one. I can say most anything I want. This concept applies in lots of places, so it's important to understand. Black comedians can poke fun of Black people. White comedians cannot. You can talk critically about your own group, but not others. Simple rule to follow. Life will be better.

In the chapters about Black people and women, for example, I try to be clear that I am talking about these things from an inherently White and male perspective. No matter how thoughtful I might be, that still matters.

The way I want to approach talking about men, and then about women in the next chapter, requires holding two key thoughts at the same time: Most men are the same, and all men are different. These are diametrically opposed concepts, but I believe they both are true.

Men are, in general, all the same. It is a bell curve for sure, with a huge number of men with similar characteristics in the middle, and as you move away from the typical, you see an increasingly smaller number of outliers in both directions. And let's say those tails on the bell curve roughly correlate with insanely toxic masculinity on one end and gentle, quiet femininity on the other. Most men are in the middle somewhere. And these traits are generally different from those that define women.

And you might be wondering why this chapter focuses on a certain kind of men, and the next chapter on a certain demographic of women. There's plenty of variation in sexuality and gender identity, so what gives? Across the entire book, I tried to think about how I was writing, what perspective I was coming from. And then I tried to make this useful regardless of identity, skin color, sexuality, or anything else.

But when it comes to talking about men in general, if you assume that a large majority of people identify as their sex assigned at birth and as heterosexual, then I am covering a huge part of the bell curve here. This big part of the bell curve is kind of the point: To talk about men in general before talking about how we're different from each other.

Another pair of opposite thoughts I need you to hold at the same time: Men are wonderful and amazing, and they are terrible and the source of almost everything that's wrong in the world.

Where am I going with all of this? Let's break it down into two parts: First, what we as men need to hear – and often be better about. Second, what women can take away from this that might help navigate, manage, and sometimes survive, us.

Let's start with that inward look:

First, try to see that our worldview is inherently male, especially White male. What does that mean? Our default views, the ones we think are broadly applicable, often are not. The things that men see as obvious and normal often are neither. In the things we value and the things we don't: these often are not the same values and experiences of the rest of the world. By seeing the world through our lens, we get it wrong a lot when we talk to people, and we get it wrong in the actions we take and don't take.

As a hard, cold, practical matter, if your default view means the most to you and you don't really care to think differently, know this: You are probably not coming across well to a huge part of the world, and it doesn't accomplish what you want effectively. The operating costs are higher than they need to be. It's inefficient.

So if I can't convince you to work on being a better human, or you're convinced you don't need any improvement, then let me argue this: It's still worth assessing your approach to the world to see whether making some adjustments to account for different perspectives makes you more successful and more efficient.

Here's an example that explains a great deal: What we value. Men typically care about high intelligence and technical things. We value occupations such as engineers, lawyers, doctors, and scientists. Also, we care about things we do with our hands, like carpenters or mechanics. We like builders, inventors, and problem-solvers. Hike-through-the-mountains-alone-with-a-knife-and-a-stick sorts of men. Men who excel in games of skill and athletics. You get the idea. We value strength. We value winning. We value success.

And lastly, at the very least, we value what we *understand.* So if you're a doula or a life coach, a counselor, really anything that seems like feelings are involved, or is vague, or doesn't have a tangible product or outcome, we're not going to value it – at least not as much as what *we* think is important.

We also tend to see ourselves and our interests as what's important in the world and everything else as secondary. Basically, the rest of the world is here to support us.

Feelings – and sharing about them – are often not a priority. It's a cliché and a stereotype here, as much as it will be in the next chapter when I say women are the opposite. But because it's how so many of us were raised, it's broadly true enough that it's important to understand in relationships and in the workplace.

Because if you need that sharing and caring in a partner, then make sure you find one who already has the traits, or be prepared to feed that need with friends and not have it in your primary relationship. And if you're the caring and sharing type, remember that when you're planning strategies and activities at work, that sharing circle might not be right for everyone.

Men are also the source of so much of the suffering in the world. We cause much of the violence, the assault, the abuse. We take; we hurt. We rationalize what we see as good for us as good for everyone, that what we want is our right to have.

That ties up with a bow an awful lot of the bad and worse we started with, so what about the good that men are?

There are lots of wonderful men in the world. Men who are wonderful for different reasons and in different ways. Men who are creative and talented, decisive and strong, mentoring and caring. Men who will give you the shirt off their backs. Men who will sacrifice everything to make sure you're OK, that you're safe.

This chapter is less about them. They can still learn and grow from this book, and they are already open to it and capable of it. But mostly, this is about the rest of the guys.

Men often complain that women seek out those who are strong, powerful, or rich. Then, this narrative continues, women complain that they don't have a partner who is caring, thoughtful and sensitive. And all the caring, thoughtful, and sensitive men say, "What did you *think* was going to happen?" And on some level, we're building a male version of the impossible standards women are held to. Men need to be rugged warrior models, who are poet lover empaths, with the skills of a mechanic mountain man farmer.

Men also feel like women have conflicting drives. The idea of security that attracts them to wealth, power, and strength. The idea of passing on your genes, a good mate in the survival of the fittest sort of way. The oft-competing idea is to have a meaningful partner who values and supports you. Women often end up with one or the other, instead of one who lands on a good spot between the two. Too many times, this means too much compromise in something that's fundamentally important in a partner who will complement you well.

Now let's change gears and talk about what women might be able to use from this. We'll start with the chapter's opening idea that we're basically big dogs that talk or large five-year-old boys.

Use these tongue-in-cheek analogies to better understand men. Then take that and use it to manage us toward making things better in relationships and in the workplace. And use these ideas to pick partners that fit with you.

Managing people, not changing them, is so much more effective and feasible. But they have to be people who are at their cores fundamentally decent enough and compatible enough for you. Because actual change happens slowly, over time, and only around the edges for lots of men.

Is he in love with any idea that's his and doesn't hear anyone else's? Help him get there on his own instead of telling him how something should be done. This is just one example, but keep in mind that broadly speaking, if you focus on what's important to you, but wrap it in the context of what's important to him (comfort, attention, praise), you can make good things happen.

It has to be sincere though, or you will feel gross and wrong (or you should anyway). This gets back to the idea that the men in your life need to be reasonably decent humans, and have things in common with you, as a starting point. If they aren't, trying to get them there from zero is a recipe for failure and suffering.

This might sound a little manipulative, but the way I am trying to frame it, it's about managing, not manipulating (which has a healthy dose of insincerity). If you do this for good, not evil, and everybody benefits, then it's just a tool that works. And if you are, in the end, speaking up and asking directly for what you want, but just doing it in a way that will be heard, I'd say that's not manipulative at all. I'd say that was finding the right way to communicate.

We spent a lot of time on how men are basically all the same – in the big part of the bell curve anyway. So let's blend in how men are all different. Not just the ones at the extremes, but even among the ones in the middle. One might be loud and shallow, another quiet and thoughtful. And as much as judging the book by its cover is often accurate, many times it's not.

The key is to take all of this and use it to make yourself better if you're a man, or to deal with men better if you're a woman. It boils down to one thing: Don't make those assumptions about who men are. Learn who we are before you judge, before you leap, before you trust.

I won't say this the same way in the next chapter, because when women *do* give men the benefit of the doubt, when they *do* avoid judging, or assuming, or lumping all of us together, the cost of being wrong can be very high. Trauma, injury, death high.

This means women have to be more cautious than men, and we need to give the space for that and accept it. We are the reason for that caution, so we need to own this.

So what *do* we do as men to be better? See All The Other Chapters. That's fundamentally what this book is about: to help you be a Decent Human Being, and if you already are, to be a better one and to learn how to deal with – or help – those who are not.

Chapter 53: About Women

Here's a multiple-choice question:

How does a middle-aged White guy write about women?

A) he doesn't
B) very carefully
C) from a particular perspective
D) poorly
E) all of the above
F) any of the above

All are probably correct, so what do I do? Write it anyway.

Here's another multiple-choice question:

Why am I writing about women?

A) to win a lifetime mansplaining award
B) to be an ally and maybe help share something important

(Please let the answer end up being B.)

What I am *not* trying to do is to tell women about women. That would be dumb and irritating. This is an attempt to help men understand some things that women already know and have been saying to us. But as men we often are not really paying attention to anything other than the things we care about. And the things we care about often are very narrowly focused on us.

Let's start with categories I call "Things Men Don't Deal With":

LOSS OF IDENTITY – Women who get married usually lose their name and adopt their spouses'. Men don't think about this because it doesn't affect them and of course, it seems just fine to them. Some women are probably happy to do it, but I suspect lots of them struggle with losing that identity and losing a connection to their own family history. For those who keep their own last name, or who go the hyphenated route, our society, traditions, and structures make that hard, sometimes awkward, sometimes a giant hassle.

SECONDARY CAREERS – It's totally normal for a woman to work and have a career. Until… Until she gets married, then her husband's career is generally the one that takes precedence. His career drives when you move and where you go. His career doesn't get slowed down or derailed by having children. And again, men don't think a lot about this because the traditional arrangement works just fine for them, and it seems normal. Sure, plenty of men will talk about it, but in the end, their perspective drives the idea that the decision the "family" makes is the right one.

DEVALUED WORK – Women are in the same careers that men are, but if you look at the professions where there are more women than men, you will likely see one or both of these trends as the percentage of women rises: Lower salaries, and an attitude toward them that shows we don't value the work as much. Next time you talk to a teacher, ask her how many times she's heard variations of questions/comments about how much time she gets off in a year, how "short" the workday is, and other things that imply it's easy. And look at how much we pay teachers in most places relative to other professions. Even when the professions are the same, women still deal with lower salaries for the same work.

DOUBLE STANDARDS – From voice tone to appearance, fitness for career, or about any activity or pursuit they're engaged in, women are patronized, questioned, challenged, second-guessed, and mocked. And it happens even more for women of color. Men certainly face unfair criticism and mocking, but for most of us, it's not a routine thing, not an encounter that can happen daily in ways small or large like it is for women.

DEVALUED SELF – How many times have you seen a woman put her needs second? If you're a woman, the answer is probably something like "too many to count." If you're a man, the answer might be something like "women do that?" Examples are everywhere, and for most of the girls, they start seeing it all around them at an early age. For most girls, it becomes their norm, or they at least accept it as "the way things are." For all the girls who bristle at this, they often face all sorts of negative reactions that mostly boil down to attempting to make them feel bad, selfish, or a failure as a woman. Girls learn that their needs are irrelevant at worst, that they come second at best. Spouses, children, parents, pretty much everyone else's needs come first. I have watched this change over the years, slowly, but change nonetheless. My kids didn't accept it as automatic as did so many who came before them. But no matter how much has changed in society, it's still built into the fabric enough to matter.

OBJECTS – "Smile for me." That's probably one of the milder offenses, but it's still an offense against women. And it only gets worse from there. Women don't say that to women. Men don't say that to other men. Too many men treat women as objects. Instead of "smile," we might as well be saying "dance for me," "dress in a way that pleases me," "turn slowly in a circle so I can look at your body, and tell you about it, and what I want to do with it." Women hear all of those things and worse. We are asking women to perform for us. We are asking them to entertain us, to pleasure us.

THREATS TO SAFETY – This happens all around the world, all throughout history, in ways small and large, bad and worse. Women and girls are assaulted and killed. Women are extorted and forced. From hidden abuse to outrageous acts in war, it happens so much that it completely changes how girls are taught to navigate the world. It looms over them, forces impossible choices between freedom and safety, and it perpetuates control by men, rules set by men, to protect them from men. The absurdity of this would be comic if the consequences weren't so damaging, so deadly.

INHERENT CONFLICT – Society wants you to be a mother, and (usually) it encourages you to have a career. And you can be great at either. But everything we do and say sets a clear expectation that we want you to do both.

So many women, by choice or not, do both. I suspect they are all exhausted. All the time. And they are beaten-down, frustrated, and often full of doubt that they are not "good enough." Too many women I know feel this way. This inherent conflict between motherhood and professional life creates this no-win scenario. It's a scenario not many men have to deal with. All of this feeds into...

IMPOSSIBLE EXPECTATIONS – There are commercials I remember as a kid telling women they could be successful at work, great mothers, and sexy hot going out at night. They could have it all. And I read about that for years, this idea of having it all. This idea of superwoman, supermom. I call BS. It's an unreasonable expectation, an impossible cultural norm. Sure, maybe you can have it all, do it all, but how many women do you know who are just flat-out exhausted pretty much all the time? How many women do you know who, at least on some level, feel like failures? We created that. Society. Men. Unreasonable and sometimes impossible standards of what women can do well on any given day, day after day. She needs to work out and look great, dress well, be a chef, keep an amazing house, raise perfect children, and dedicate more than full time to a demanding career. It sounds ridiculous, but we see it expressed or implied all the time in marketing, pop culture – all over the place. As women entered the workforce, but still carried the workload for home and children, the men said, grudgingly, "OK, you can work, we'll take the extra income, but don't inconvenience me." Even as society rapidly shifts toward exposing and addressing these impossible expectations, it's still there. A system-wide, society-level judgment of her choices. If she picks home over work, or work over home, or her happiness over forcing herself to meet an appearance expectation, or puts her needs first, she pays for it. Nothing comes to women free of judgment, free of cost.

UNBALANCED COMPROMISE – Relationships are about compromise. That's not unreasonable. In relationships though, women tend to compromise more than men. They compromise their wants, needs, and interests. The things you do, places you go, movies you watch, the hobbies and activities that entertain and make you happy: those tend to be driven by the men. The places men tend to compromise end up being either inconsequential or begrudging. A stereotypical example: He expects you to be interested in his sports attending/watching/playing, but will get dragged to the ballet you like once a year or so – and he'll expect a trophy for it. This imbalance is created and sustained by the secondary roles women can end up in. Even as newer generations reject this imbalance, they are still punished on some level for that demand for balance, for independence especially.

LACK OF SOVEREIGNTY – I was thinking about a lack of independence and of respect when I was drafting this chapter. Then I heard about the idea of "sovereignty" for women. To me, the term defines what nations demand from each other. Traditionally, that's how the word is used. And it strikes me as an inherently male view because I have no reason to think about the concept in other contexts. As a nation, we want to be taken seriously, to be respected, to be free to make decisions as we see fit – and free from others making decisions for us. We want to be safe in our borders and free from invasion and assault. We want a seat at the table and respect for what we bring to it. We want to be accepted free of assumptions about what we can and can't do. We don't want to be patronized or treated with condescension. Now replace "nation" with "women" and it seems to me that it captures nicely a huge range of ideas and issues into one word.

In all of these categories, I suspect most people would agree there's been a ton of progress. More men are open to more balanced partnerships, and many more women are accepting no less than equal partnerships. But I doubt very many women would say it's all good now. Every story my mother told me of her experience in the 1970s corporate world has a more subtle version that can be told today. There's a huge amount written about all of these ideas, but the takeaway from all of these short summaries: Watch the things you say and do, and check your own thinking. Don't contribute to the problem.

Women are all the things I said about men in the last chapter: creative and talented, decisive and strong, mentoring and caring. But when you think of the traits typically associated with women, others tend to stand out: caring, sharing, empathy, support, listening, and kindness. A lot of this can be described simply by the higher levels of emotional intelligence women often possess. Women more highly value friendships, connections, depth, empathy, thoughtfulness, caring, and feelings.

Which gets us back to this idea: Men and women are all the same. Men and women are completely different. Women are all the same. Women are all unique. How you feel about these four statements; how you react to the ideas, has a lot to do with you, who you're with, and with the time, place, and context. And all the statements are true, and they all are not.

Again, just like the bell curve of men, there is a big group in the middle. A group that's all the same, and at the same time, all different. And out on one tail of the curve are the women who couldn't care less about feelings, just want to get the job done, grab a shot of whisky, and go out and play. And on the other end are women who value the most traditional definitions of femininity and nurturing things above all others. Being a wife and mother to the exclusion of everything else is really the sum of it.

We make the mistake all the time looking at women as a single monolithic thing. But there are as many variations as you can come up with, not one-size-fits-all, except maybe when it comes to fair treatment and safety.

If we start there, the first thing we do is say stop and don't make assumptions. Assuming the woman you are talking to fits any particular part of the bell curve is efficient and often right, and it is always the wrong way to do it. You don't know what matters to her until you take the time to find out.

"What do women want?" I hear the men asking. That's not the right question. A better one is "what does *this* woman want?" And the answer is "I don't know, try asking her."

"Some women like to be pursued," the men say. Well, sure, some do. And some like to do the pursuing, some like neither, and some just want to be left alone. Some just don't like *you.* That's an important concept to remember.

No one is required to like you.

"How do I know how to act, what to do?" the men ask. You don't. So be you, approach gently, and learn when to back off and that no means no. These are incredibly important man skills.

When it comes to men "making the first move," it's important to understand the weird and difficult spot we are putting women in. If they treat us like predators who are likely a danger to them, then it stifles exploration and discovery of new relationships. And if they treat you like you are genuine and a Decent Human Being, they can end up assaulted or dead.

I know making the first move is what's been expected of men in our culture basically forever. I know change is hard, as is giving up control. But if you put yourself in women's shoes for a minute and see from their eyes the history of violence and assault from men that didn't "seem the type," then maybe you can do something to make it easier for them. First, know they are in a tough spot and asking them to be alone with you early on is just a bad idea. It puts them in a place where they have to make potentially life-or-death decisions.

Why do that to anyone? So you have to learn to let them drive where that goes or doesn't, and just get used to it. It requires taking the back seat more often. It's a skill that's important to learn for other reasons too (see Chapter 15, Taking the Back Seat).

And let me pause to say the same thing about women that I said about men in the last chapter: If you assume that a large majority of people identify as their sex assigned at birth and as heterosexual, then I am covering a huge part of the bell curve here. This big part of the bell curve is kind of the point: to frame talking about women in general, and at the same time, talking about them as individuals who are unique.

This isn't to say that everyone who identifies anywhere else on the spectrums of gender and sexuality isn't relevant, isn't important. Everyone is. It's that large majorities of men and women identify as their sex assigned at birth and are attracted to the opposite sex.

So we start there to try to capture all the things that are relevant to most people, then I try to cover in chapters on gender and sexuality the additional challenges people face when they don't conform to outdated, "traditional" notions of "normal."

My mother was an executive in the early high-tech industry developing in New Hampshire when I was a kid. She told me a story that took root in my kid head: In a meeting where she was the only woman, when it was time for coffee, they asked her to get it.

Women are often the ones who plan the events, gatherings, and parties. They get the cake and the card at the office. And that's great. But what do we do? We assume it's a woman's job and assign it to them not knowing whether that particular woman would rather have you do it while she runs the meeting. On one hand, a lot of that has changed since then, on the other hand, too much still hasn't.

So much of this negative behavior I write about men as it relates to women seems to be changing, some of it rapidly. It's encouraging to see how the men who are my daughter's friends seem to be more balanced and better humans. But I wonder sometimes if that's just who she has surrounded herself with. Bottom line is we're making progress, but there is still so much more to do.

I look at it this way: Men are the only ones who think we've fixed our problems treating women unequally. Just like White people are the only ones who think we've dealt with racism. Or heterosexual, cis-gendered people are the only ones who think that everyone else is now treated decently in society.

Let's dive into the world of double standards for a bit. Or at least what could appear to be a double standard. You see lots written about how women bring something different to leadership. To me, this "difference" makes sense because not many people would argue that men and women are generally the same.

Bringing new and different traits to leadership, new and different perspectives, should strike everyone as healthy and desirable. It *should* anyway. I look at gaining new skills and perspectives in our collective leadership as a benefit of broadening the access and participation of women in leadership roles they have traditionally been excluded from.

Not that we need a reason to address this inequality beyond simply addressing an inequality. Anyway, the narrative goes something like this: Women bring caring, understanding, empathy, an ability to listen. Lots of people would agree and applaud this. If I then say men bring strength and decisiveness, an ability to make quick decisions without letting emotions get in the way, I would not be so applauded. You can say women are "better" or bring value in some way, but not men. Why?

One of the arguments is that when men discriminate there is an inherent imbalance of power. It's the same scenario as when White people discriminate against Black people. The thinking continues that it is the imbalance of power that carries the damage. So when women do things that would be considered discriminatory if men did them it's therefore OK.

Another example: A friend has been working under intense pressure with a huge workload and a ridiculous number of hours put in day in and day out. She's pretty beat down. There's a woman who works for her who's in the same boat, and my friend's boss is a woman, who is also going through the same things.

So they decide to gather on a Friday night, have a drink, and just decompress. This sounds to me like a great idea, a healthy idea. But they excluded the men. If I flip this around, and the women were excluded, it would be a problem.

I go back to the same rationale as the leadership difference question: Men have traditionally excluded women from essentially all groups, gatherings and activities that mattered for the conduct of business, for the growth of wealth and power. That's why, in the simplest terms, it's not OK to do this as we work to address this inequity.

Women doing the same thing, you could argue, doesn't carry the same baggage and damage to men. There is another argument that when women and minority groups are marginalized, the process of undoing that damage creates an environment where women and others can and should band together to support each other and learn from their experiences navigating this transition.

Sometimes I hear people, men usually, taking issue with groups for women. Because, they say, we can't have a group just for men. If I could do stand-up comedy (and I can't), I would do a routine that said, "Well, there is an all-male organization out there, it's called 'everything'." It's the same for most any group created to support and empower women: The version for men is whatever we already had in society. Most of those groups traditionally excluded women. Sports and fellowship clubs, business and civic organizations, you get the idea. Even though these groups now accept women as members, more than a few are still dominated by men either in focus, operation, or membership.

If we were talking about race and this same concept, I'd do another joke at my failed stand-up routine when people complain that we can have an NAACP, but not an organization to advance White people. It would go something like: "We do have an NAAWP, it's called 'America'."

One more example: There's a female CEO I know who is openly proud of the all-female staff at her organization. But at another well-known organization in my community, the leadership team is all male, and all White for that matter. No one cheers that (at least not openly). Both of these groups serve everyone, not just men or women.

It's interesting to me to think about this and to talk about this in an effort to learn. Why is it different? The traditional power imbalance? A growing culture of women nurturing and supporting other women in leadership, a culture that suffers from some missteps and growing pains, and some grumpy male backlash? Perspective difference, whether it's a good difference or not?

I don't know the answers here in any of these examples. These are big and complex questions we face in our society. I will end with this thought: If we accept that there is no double standard here – or that there is, but it's OK – because of the reasons (or similar ones) that I outlined, then it would make sense to me for women to take the lead on this. That a practical path would be for women to be mindful that there's a line between supporting other women, for example, and doing the same things they want to move away from. And that it's up to them to decide where that line is – and to stay on the right side of it.

The same goes with the example in how we describe positive traits and qualities women bring to leadership: If we can talk about those as good and desirable things, and we should, then we need to get comfortable talking about what men bring to the table that *is* good and valuable, so we can figure out how best to support each other.

All of this comes down to, like so much that's good in us as humans, awareness and empathy. And for men especially, taking the time to make sure we have these traits, these skills, so we can be an ally and not the problem. So we can learn to walk in other people's shoes.

Chapter 54: Out Front

In 2020, we saw just about every company and organization, large and small, writing heartfelt messages in social media posts, newsletters, emails, and website home pages. This started during the pandemic, and then continued because of our nation's newest racial wounds. Initially, I kept my own feelings confined to a circle of family and friends. As important as these issues are to me, they didn't seem directly relevant to my data and coaching work.

But the realization dawned that two of the most important things to me in my coaching and analytics work – leadership and data – are key to being part of the solution. That found a natural home in this book, and we start here with leadership, and talk about how data is relevant to this idea in Chapter 66, The Pool.

Why leadership? That one is pretty easy. Lead by example. It's almost always the right answer. In how you conduct business, and how you treat customers, clients and workers. It's the right answer outside of the workplace, too.

I've watched, studied, and learned about culture, society, politics, leadership, and data all of my adult life. And I've read and seen plenty that show me we have problems with race and gender in our society. So what's different now? The Me Too and Black Lives Matter movements highlighted two things: it's all worse and more widespread than I knew. And it's not enough to be a good person, and to treat women and people of color with dignity and respect.

What's different now is that we see the need to be more active. To use our resources, knowledge, experience, influence, and connections – whatever those are for each of us – to *do* something.

There are so many ways to be active. Do a little digging and find what fits best for you. Some examples:

- Read articles or books by people who research or advocate in these areas to educate yourself
- Lift up someone else's voice
- Review your own work or writing for inclusive language
- Advocate for resources for people of color and women in the workplace
- Get involved with a diversity effort in your workplace, or find an advocacy organization to join.

For all those who lead, or who aspire to be leaders, it's time to take a step back before you take one forward. Do a quick self-check and remember:

- It's not about you
- Make sure you are really listening to others
- Get out of your comfort zone with people and places
- Learn
- And then, *do* something.

Chapter 55: Free Speech Isn't Free

This chapter is short. Simple. But the idea is important. American society has a cherished and long-held belief in free speech. The problem we run into in our modern world comes in two forms: a general misunderstanding of what our rights are, and a collective struggle drawing a line between free speech, and speech that isn't OK.

The "misunderstanding" part is easiest to clarify. The First Amendment of the U.S. Constitution guarantees the right to free speech. In a nutshell, it says the government cannot punish you for what you say. You are free to criticize the government and most anything else without fear of retribution. Throughout history, including now, you could be killed, beaten, or thrown in jail for saying anything negative about the ruler of your nation. Our Founding Fathers wanted to fix that. And they did. Nicely.

Here's where our knowledge of civics falls apart: The government cannot punish you for your speech. However, that doesn't mean your speech is free from consequences. In most cases, your boss can fire you for saying things they feel reflect poorly on the company. Society can turn you into an outcast; it can turn its collective back on you.

I could say Kanye West is vastly overrated. I could say Taylor Swift peaked a long time ago. I won't say that. But I could. And society could ban me from the in-group and publicly chew a new hole in my butt (figuratively, hopefully). It would be my right to say those things *and* society's right to react as it saw fit.

Too often I see people raise free speech as an issue when someone gets fired, loses customers at their business, or is ostracized from their community. In none of those situations was your right to free speech violated. As long as the government does not punish you for speaking out, your rights are intact.

And a small side note: There are limits to our rights, places where the government has a say in it. The classic is you can't yell fire in a crowded theater when there is no fire, because speech such as this creates a high risk of harm in the likely ensuing stampede. The other typical scenario is when your speech incites violence against others. This is a vast oversimplification of First Amendment law, but the idea is there.

There are also limits outside of government where you can be sued for libel or slander by another private party for intentionally false and harmful things you write or say. But generally, you are entitled to voice your opinion.

The other place we struggle is defining acceptable speech. Free speech rights are also there to protect ideas we disagree with. People have every right to say things that you find awful. We are in a period of intense debate on the limits of speech. Some people want to ban speech they see as hate, the kind of speech they see as creating the conditions for violence. Others say it's repugnant – but protected – if it's not advocating violence against someone or some group. The difficulty is finding where that line is.

Government, the courts, the media, interest groups, corporations, and the rest of us are all trying to figure this out, and my general belief and hope is that over time, we get to somewhere better with our rights intact.

Remember, your speech is free, but that doesn't mean it won't cost you.

Chapter 56: Religion

When it comes to religion, my general advice, my best advice, is don't be a jerk about it.

Here in the United States most people identify as Christian. That's pretty straightforward, and that's where straightforward ends. There are plenty of Christian denominations, and varying levels of adherence to them. And in addition to people of the Jewish faith here, increasingly in our diversifying society, more people are Muslim, Hindu, or any of the other religions of the world.

No matter how hostile or cynical you might feel toward organized religion and what has transpired throughout history – even recent history for some – there are so many other stories of churches and their congregations doing work that no one else will do. People trying to take care of the least among us day in and day out. The homeless, the addicted, people with severe mental illnesses, ex-cons, today's version of biblical lepers that most of us avoid.

On the other side of the coin are those who proclaim that people who don't believe what they believe are going to hell, or that other gods are false, or that only certain behaviors are acceptable. And that is probably meant genuinely, sincerely, and not unkindly. But that's not how it comes across.

It's quick and easy to paint it as all good or all bad, but it's complicated, like everything else. Avoid the easy judgment. (See Chapter 59, Nonbinary World).

Some faiths are inward-looking, and for some it is a primary mission to spread the word to others. And for a lot of people, hearing talk of faith and of actions driven by faith can seem strange. Remind yourself that while it might be strange to you, for those who believe, it's earnest and genuine.

Faith is key here. Once you understand that religion is about faith, there's really nothing for you to declare real, or try to convince someone they are wrong about. Or to insist someone who doesn't share your faith, well, that they simply must. That means you don't challenge someone to defend their belief. You don't challenge someone to prove their religion is valid, or that God exists.

When you meet people, they could be from the same religion as you are, or a different one, or have no religion at all. They could have varying beliefs about their religion. We often assume someone we meet shares the same perspective we have about things. Don't. (See Chapter 46, Perspective.)

Think before you speak and err on the side of silence, especially in the workplace. This is not about being stifled; it's about being respectful, being thoughtful, sometimes about just not being a jerk.

One of the pillars of American society is freedom of religion. In the U.S. Constitution, that means we are all free to worship how we choose, that the government won't favor one belief over another, or have an official government religion. And when we talk about society, politics, and the issues we face, that doesn't mean religion should have no role. It is right and proper for people of faith to express what they believe and to advocate for policies that align. If you don't like what a particular church is saying, don't go there. If you don't like that a business owner champions his faith through his work policies, don't work there, don't patronize that business. And if you don't agree with the political goals of national faith groups, then oppose them in your own ways.

We are a nation and a people built on ideas of tolerance and freedom, and they are ideas we must all protect, regardless of our beliefs.

So, if you believe in God. That's great. If you don't, that's great too. If you go to church or don't, if you live the way your faith teaches, or don't, well, you get the idea.

Faith is personal. Faith is for families and friends. Don't run your mouth on social media or in the office about what God is or isn't; about which faith or denomination is "right" or "wrong." This is different than sharing with the world what you believe. It's about doing it with respect and kindness to others.

Those are wonderful and weighty questions best left to academic environments, and they are discussions for family and close friends, too. Because they are important, profound, and meaningful.

Remind yourself that what you think is just that: what you think. Remind yourself that it's easy to hurt someone with loose talk about what you have decided is or isn't real or genuine.

PART V: Leveling Up

We've been through so much together in Human Training. More than 50 chapters on so very many topics. We looked at ways to see yourself, ways to be a better you, and ways to help keep your sanity when dealing with all the people out there who seem determined to drive you crazy.

So let's take one more dive into the waters, this time looking at ways to level up, to up your game, to gain that extra wisdom and perspective that will move you from Decent Human Being to Walking Wizard of Wonderful.

Chapter 57: Evolve

If you look at your parents, or really most any adult who is older than you are, you often see people who don't have any taste in fashion or music, or really in anything. They are so not cool. There are two big reasons for this, well lots of reasons, but two big ones.

First, to those in the latest generation, you know everything. You are on top of the newest trends and technology, the current lingo and ways of thinking. You are connected to the current activities of life and its entertainment. Hell, you create the trends. You are awesome and complex, and you carry a weight of our times that is so very different, and well, heavy. And your parents and their generation are basically clueless. Here's the deal: This is true. You are right. But before you get too smug about it, this has been true for thousands of years, with *every* generation. So don't get too full of yourself. It's just a natural cycle.

The second – and the one that matters more – is a cautionary tale: As life gets busier and busier after we're done with school, especially when you add marriage and kids to the mix, we focus our energies where we need them: our partners, our children, our careers, our homes. This can push out almost anything else, including all that time we used to spend keeping up with the latest in music, art, technology, fashion, movies, books, actors, and well, you get the idea.

Life can be triage. Just getting through each day is a nonstop exercise in barely contained chaos that ends with your exhausted head on a pillow. Maybe you hold onto one or two things, like playing a sport you love, or reading or music, or a hobby that gives you much satisfaction. Something. Maybe.

You end up with what looks like throwback taste. Your knowledge of music basically freezes after high school or college when you don't keep up anymore, so eventually you are listening to "oldies," and you didn't even see it coming. Your taste in clothes might have been good after high school or college, but again, fashion and trends keep moving and you don't, so you start to look dated.

And then that triage that is life with kids and/or a singular focus on career makes you messy, frumpy, out of shape, disconnected with life, and all too often, disconnected from your partner. If your relationship survives raising those ungrateful know-it-all little monsters, and many don't, you might be in that lucky group of partners that rediscover their passions – together – and have wonderful empty-nest years. Or, you split up and try to figure out a new life.

OK, so after all that, what was the point of this? Why is this chapter called "Evolve"?

Because you can fix this. You have that power. And it's simple. Not always easy, but it's simple: Evolve. Make it a habit. Make it a conscious effort. I promise it will be worth it.

If you don't have kids yet, great, then just take a look at your life and make sure you are, you know, living. Make sure you're not coming home every night, eating, planting your butt in front of the TV, and repeating the next day. And on the weekends, make sure you're not just taking care of things around the home, and maybe even doing that one thing, like watching sports, or playing sports, or whatever it is.

This is a trap. Run from it.

Hang out with friends. Make new ones. Find people who are different from you. Go somewhere. Do something. Check out a movie that's well-reviewed but not generally your taste. Watch a documentary. Try it. Subscribe to some sort of long-form writing like *The Atlantic* or *The New Yorker*, or whatever suits your tastes. Read a book. Do it. If you read one book a month, just one a month, you'll be light-years ahead in so many ways. You'll be smarter, happier, more interesting, more thoughtful. Most people don't really read at all. And it shows.

Do you like lagers or IPAs? Learn about porters and stouts. Is white wine your thing? Explore reds. When it comes to food and drink and music and art and technology, we often don't like what we don't understand, or we formed an opinion long ago and never bothered to challenge it again. It can be helpful when trying new things to explore a little first, read a little, talk to your friends. Maybe when you first tried red wine, it was a terrible one, or even a good one, but not your style. Learn a bit, then you'll know what to try next. Try most anything. See what fits.

Try some new music. It's never been easier. And whether you love to shop or hate it, pay a bit of attention to what people are wearing and just find some things that you like the look of and try them. Like music, it's never been easier to try new things. Be ruthless with your clothes. Get rid of things. Let them go. If you get one new thing every month or so – that's it, just one – you'll be free of that trap. You'll be the adult who rocks through every age, and you'll be happier. All you have to do is keep your eyes open as you swim through life.

I should point out here, in response to the sputters and eye rolls: No, you don't have to care about fashion, or be an expert in the latest music, or really the latest anything. You just need to pay enough attention to these things, pay attention to you, so that you keep learning and growing.

Another part of our lives where we just give up? What we look like. Update your hairstyle. That's the easy part. The hard one, the really hard one, is the frumpy mom look and the dad bod. They creep up on us because we devote all of our time and energy to work and family. Here's the big secret: Don't devote everything to your kids or your job or both. Raising children is probably the single most important thing most of us will do, but don't put yourself and your relationship on hold for 20 years. You can balance all of this. I promise you, you really can.

This is not a diet or exercise book, but the three things we do that probably matter the most for our health: We eat junk, we eat more than we need, and we sit around. So take baby steps: Start thinking about how much you are eating and dial it back a little. Start thinking about one little thing you can ditch. Just one. Soda, maybe. Potato chips. Something. And get out of the desk chair, get off the couch, and do something. Go for a walk. Anything. Habits form when we repeat them. And making small changes is so much easier than big commitments. Do these three little things.

And to you, the youngest of the readers: Don't get too smug and judgy about all of this. And don't be mean about it. Your time is coming.

Chapter 58: No, YOU'RE Biased!

Take a BuzzFeed quiz that promises to tell you how smart you are, and when it says you are a budding Einstein, you nod, smile, and think about how insightful and talented the people who designed the quiz must be. And if that same quiz tells you to go back to living under the bridge with the other trolls and that your best option for work is smashing rocks together, you will be angry and dismiss the quiz as silly nonsense.

Bias is pre-wired in us as humans and trained into us as we go along. Zoom out to the societal level and we see people routinely dismissing facts because they conflict with their beliefs. Being aware of bias is a critical part of using data and information in productive ways.

Bias is all over the place. We like pretty things and think they are better inside because of what they look like on the outside. We like people who like us. We like people who like the same things we do. We like people who look like us. (See Chapter 45, Groups.)

An example from the data nerd world: Many studies published in technical and scientific journals are the ones that showed *something*. Most of the studies that turned up nothing are still interesting to science, but not to the publishing world. That astounding new finding might have been just random "noise" in the data, not relevant "signal," if you also saw a bunch of research that didn't show anything.

And we even have bias in things such as health. With countless claims, seemingly endless fads, to choose from, let's pick one: People who eat fish oil are healthier. I mean, sure, the oil could be doing something useful, but the research might not have accounted for the fact that people who eat fish oil might be different – or doing different things – in ways that explain why they are healthier.

There's a wide range of biases, some more common than the others. We dive into a few in other chapters because they are so pervasive, and highlight some of the many others here:

- Confirmation – We started with this: We accept what confirms our views and ignore or reject what doesn't
- In-Group – We believe things from people we know or who are like us
- Self-Serving – Bad things that happen to us are because "stuff happens" or because someone else failed. It's not my fault. But bad things that happen to others are because they failed. Definitely their fault
- Anchoring – When we latch onto one initial idea and base all decisions that come after on that thing, whether it was true or not
- Status Quo – Things are good the way they are, and change is bad.

What can you do in the face of all of this? Three things: First, try to think like a scientist. If the data indicates something to be true, especially when there are lots of data from different people and different sources, accept it. Be open to the possibility that it's wrong, but until that's shown, allow it as your current understanding.

Second, try to keep in the front of your mind that we like data that validate our beliefs – and we dislike data that challenge them. So take that piece of information and use it to ask these questions: Why do I accept or reject this information? What do I know that allows me to do that?

And third, the world tries to force binary thinking on us all the time. Something is one way or another. Reject this. Firmly. In most cases, an issue is a spectrum, and your point of view will likely fall somewhere on it. (See Chapter 59, Nonbinary World.)

Bias is both hardwired into us and trained into us. The best thing we can do to overcome it is to be aware of it so we can find ways to see around it to get a clearer picture.

Getting to know your own perspective and how it influences you is probably the biggest one. Because of that, it gets its own treatment. (See Chapter 46, Perspective.)

Knowing your biases – and the ones likely influencing those around you – can help you be a better leader, a stronger part of the team. You know better what to count, what to discount, what matters, and what doesn't. Understanding bias leads to the right questions. It helps you be open to new information – even when you think you already are.

Chapter 59: Nonbinary World

Everything is yes or no, black and white, for or against. Black Lives Matter or Blue Lives Matter. Government is incompetent; entrepreneurs are flawless and perfect Americans. The list is endless. You are not allowed a nuanced opinion in this worldview.

We tend to think this way because it's easier, and simpler, and because it's what the talking heads in the media world feed us.

My suggestion is to resist this binary view of the world because it's usually unhelpful, often wrong, and sometimes dangerous. So much of what matters to us is a spectrum. I've tried to make the case for that in other places in the book for things like sexuality and gender. But it holds true all over the place.

Politics is a prime example. The nuance on an issue a modern politician is allowed to have exists only within the context of whatever their party says. Republicans favor tax cuts. You might be allowed to debate how big of a cut, but you can't say they are bad or not needed. Democrats believe in gun control. You might be allowed to debate how much is needed or how to address it, but reject the need? Nope. In either party, on just about any issue, you are treated like a heretic. It is just not allowed to deviate from the party orthodoxy. Go along or be sidelined and ostracized by your own people.

American history is a shining city on the hill. American history is fraught with injustice, brutality, and colonialism.

The Founding Fathers were sexist racists. The Founding Fathers were heroes.

The U.S. is becoming an increasingly diverse place, and this is a wonderful thing. The U.S. is losing its identity and heritage.

The list goes on.

My answer is going to sound simplistic, but it's this: Push back. You have to do it gently and with respect, but push back. In small steps. In little ways. Resist the binary view. Every time you can get away with a little bit of nuance, a little bit of spectrum, we all win.

And work on yourself too, because part of why we take these views is because it's easy. Nuance takes work; it takes homework. It takes time and effort to learn about the world. It's so much easier to grab some takeaway, put your feet up, and binge-watch TV or dive into a video game.

This work becomes part of the basic adulting that makes you a competent human. And yes, adulting is work. It's especially a chore for a lot of us who might not be naturally as interested in all the things going on in the world. But do the minimum work to succeed as an adult; do a little bit more to round you out as a Decent Human Being.

Chapter 60: That Sounds Right

How often do you read or hear something and just accept it? It sounds right; it fits what you already think and believe about the world. It can be subtle; we don't even notice that we do it.

Did a politician just say or do something really bad? It depends on whether you agree with their politics in general. If you do, then you'd probably mostly write it off as not a big deal, blown out of proportion, or maybe even false. If it's someone from the other side, well then, whatever they did was terrible, and you can't understand why they aren't in jail yet.

I talk about bias in Chapter 58 but pull out pieces of it in other chapters because it has so many facets that affect us in so many ways.

This one is about confirmation bias: a tendency to seek out or accept, *uncritically,* information that supports something you already believe.

You minimize, ignore, or forget the bad stuff you read or hear about something you believe, and you remember the good stuff. People will cue into things that matter to them and dismiss the things that don't.

I read a line once that said an idealogue was someone whose worldview was unchanged by new information. I always liked this wording. Short and to the point. And as we moved into an era of hyper-partisan politics, binary arguments, and firmly divided outlooks, it rings true ever more painfully.

What I am challenging you to do is this: Whenever you hear something you agree with, ask yourself whether it holds up, whether the facts support it. Go look it up. Check. Use multiple resources. And when you hear something you disagree with, ask yourself why. And then go look it up. Just because we don't like someone, or we disagree with them in general, doesn't mean they are wrong. They might be, but it's not a given.

This is what we need to train ourselves about. Don't let your dismissal of anything that doesn't support your point of view be automatic.

And if people important to you are like this, don't try to beat them into submission with facts and your superior brain. Ask questions. Gently. With curiosity.

When you ask questions that have an undertone of "what you are saying is stupid and wrong, and also you are stupid and wrong," then the questions don't come across as genuine. Try something that sounds more like this: "That's interesting; I hadn't heard that before. Tell me more." Or, "Where can I read more about that?"

It comes down to looking harder at both the things you want to accept and the things you want to reject. Work to make sure they both deserve it.

Chapter 61: The Power of Numbers

An absurd thing in my collection of absurd things is a retired safe from a bank ATM. I needed to move it to a new office, which meant rolling it down a ramp on a heavy-duty furniture dolly. Since I wasn't sure how much weight I'd be holding back and whether it would crush me, I did a little math to calculate the force it would have given the weight and the incline (ignoring friction). The result was a low enough number that the plan could proceed.

That's using numbers in everyday life. Lots of these applications are routine for many of us, such as comparing unit costs between items at the grocery. What I am encouraging here is a broader view of where numbers come in handy, which is just about everywhere if you're open to it.

A few years back during one of the crazy-high gas-price cycles, I worked with another human who had just purchased a giant SUV. All of a sudden, the cost to fill this thing up went through the roof, and she decided to dump it for a fuel-efficient small car.

I suggested she look at the numbers first. Her big SUV was a new purchase, so she was upside-down on the value compared to what she owed. And the market for these guzzlers was pretty weak because no one wanted them. So she was going to take a big hit on the sale. Then the cost of the new, smaller car was through the roof because the demand was high. No one was going to give her a deal.

The next step was to take the likely difference in what this transaction would cost and see how long it would take in fuel savings to recover it. Cutting her fuel spending in half still meant it was something like 10 years to just break even, and that was assuming prices stayed that high, which was unlikely. The data said it would cost her far less to ride out the short-term crisis.

But spending more than $100 to fill her tank each time just burned her soul, and so she sold it anyway. I like this example because it's a use of numbers that would have a real impact in everyday life. And it's one that shows sometimes we take a different path even when the data clearly points another way.

We're human after all, and sometimes other things are more important, including those that might not make sense on paper. But the numbers were there, and a walk through them would have saved a lot of money and headache for her if she could have gotten past the emotion.

Let's dig a little into other ways to use numbers. For example, let standard deviation – my favorite – help you know whether something is typical or not. If a room is full of people who are on average 5 feet, 8 inches tall, and you know that the standard deviation is 3 inches (Excel will be delighted that you asked, and it will happily tell you this number), then you know that most people are between 5'5" and 5'11" (ranging from 3 inches less than the average to 3 inches more). Standard deviation is just the average difference from the average.

You now know that most people are plus or minus 3 inches from that average (one standard deviation that captures about 68%), and that almost everyone is plus or minus 6 inches from the average (two standard deviations that capture about 95%). If someone is 5 feet or someone is 7 feet, you know that in this case, it's not typical.

Why is this useful? It's one way to look at data and assess whether something really *is* a problem before you start throwing resources at it. If your sales numbers are down a bit, but it's very close to your average, it's entirely possible, likely even, that it's normal variation. Still a bummer maybe, but probably no reason to fire people or otherwise get all worked up and have everyone drop everything to start hunting for a nonexistent problem. Math can sound complex, and lots of it is. But so much is accessible to us – and useful.

Let a simple regression equation help you forecast what's likely to happen next given what's already happened. These are easy to do in a spreadsheet, and the math is essentially the "y=mx+b" we learned in high school as the slope of a line. If you want to be the office wizard and predict sales numbers for the next month, dig into using it for forecasting.

That same regression equation can be used to look at how much one thing varies with another. "Varies with" is important. Really important. Correlation does not imply causation. That's a big one. In other words, just because something is *related* to another thing, doesn't mean it *causes* the other thing. It might, but it's not automatic.

There are lots of sick people in Florida, and there are lots of doctors. So doctors make people sick, right? A regression equation would probably show a strong correlation between the number of sick people and the number of doctors.

It's likely, for example, that doctors go where they are needed, and Florida has lots of retirees who have more medical needs than younger people. After all, when I was tricked into moving here, one of the first things I heard was "Welcome to God's waiting room."

The regression equation math is not hard, though it can look scary, and it's easy enough to get a spreadsheet to do it for you. Getting our brains to think about what's going on, and to make sure it makes sense, is what's hard.

The more you understand about the power of numbers, the more you can cut through folklore, bias, and assumptions. "Streaks," for example, are generally meaningless. And just about everything that is amazing (or terrible) will drift back toward average over time. Probabilities are not hard to calculate and can be useful in helping you make decisions. It can be as easy as this: Flipping a coin is 50% likely to be heads, and flipping two heads in a row is 50% x 50% = 25%. Once you know how likely an outcome is, you can assign a weight to how good or bad that is for you, and come up with real ways to measure risk and decide which course of action is best for you.

"Average" is another good example – and one you might have heard about more than once. If you put Elon Musk and 9 random people in a room, add up their individual net worth, and then divide by 10, you'll get a number that is the average, the mean in this case. It's correct, but of course misleading. If you take the middle of the pack in those values, you get the median, a much more useful number in this situation.

Mean is a more precise number but is influenced by extremes. Median goes for the middle and doesn't care about extremes. And we can throw in the odd-ball sibling: Mode. That's just the one that happens the most in the data. (What's the modal value of cars in the airport parking lots? Gray Camrys?)

Mean, median, and mode are all averages, they are all "measures of central tendency." It's a level-up skill to know the difference among them and which one makes sense in which context.

Now add the idea of "reasonableness checks" to your mental tool box. When you're working with any number, no matter how simple the use, pause and ask yourself, "Does this make sense?"

I was working with federal criminal data and noticed the average age of these felons was like 70 or something. My reasonableness check kicked that one out and I started digging. I mean, it was possible I suppose, just not likely. I thought crime was a young man's game. I discovered a bunch of "999" values (for missing data) had been included in my math. It was an easy fix, and this extra validation check saved me a lot of embarrassment.

If you calculated the net worth in the previous example and came up with a number that ends in "billions," you then ask yourself "Hey, does it make sense that the average net worth in the U.S. is in the billions?" Then you can go look up a couple of things to give you some confidence that your number is good, or things that make you question it and dig into your underlying numbers a bit more. This one general question will save you a lot of headache down the road.

Income is another sort of data that might pop up as an example. Is the number you read about family income or individual? Is it national or local? Has regional cost of living been taken into account?

Or when you compare dollar amounts across time, have they been adjusted for inflation? In 1950, the purchasing power of $50,000 was a whole lot more than it is today. Inflation matters. My first job after college amounted to about $15 an hour. That was enough to live in a small apartment in Washington, D.C., without roommates. Not well and not by much, but it was enough. Today, we argue about $15 as a minimum wage.

The takeaway from all of this? Ask just enough, dig just enough, to be comfortable that you aren't being played, manipulated, or even just unintentionally being shown a picture that's not accurate.

Look at all the marketing pitches to put solar on the roof of your house, as just one in an ocean of examples. They are full of savings. But when you start digging, lots of the claims are based on using roughly zero power from your local utility.

Since the sun doesn't always shine, and you're likely not using a battery system to store the power for later, your savings are likely to be some part of your electric bill, not the whole thing. When you lower the return on your investment, it makes the time to recover that investment so much longer. And then it starts to make less sense for lots of people.

Now I hear the keyboard warriors wailing away at an angry response. Calm down people, this is in *general*; it's an example. Yes, if you generate such an amazing surplus, *and* you live in an area where the utility gladly pays you for all your excess power, *and* it doesn't charge you a hefty monthly fee to remain connected to the grid they have to keep up whether you use any power or not, sure, it *can* work. And yes, you might do it because it makes your soul happy. That's not the point. This is an argument to always look at the numbers to see whether they make sense.

Many of us ignore numbers and data because they don't seem relevant to our everyday lives. And many others avoid numbers and data because they don't like or don't get math.

Take this chapter as a gentle nudge to look into it a little. There are a ton of sites just a Google search away waiting to help. The pieces we can use to make life easier are within reach.

And too many people make the useful math seem too complicated. Ignore them. They have a problem, not you.

Chapter 62: Go Look It Up

We are efficient creatures. We naturally strive to conserve our internal resources. This also at times makes us lazy. How are these different?

Laziness has a cost to you, to others, or both. You are asking others to care for you, to take care of you. Or you are just getting along without something because it's good enough not to bother. This costs you; it's just a price you're willing to pay (or don't realize you're paying).

Efficiency is minimizing the load on you and on others by doing things more effectively. We strive to limit ourselves to doing only what makes sense and what is worth the value of the time put into it.

I am making a plea to be efficient, not lazy.

Do your homework. Read the manual. Stop winging it.

If you want to *know* an answer, go look it up. Don't ask others, don't guess, don't wing it. Having all the information of the world at your fingertips, well, it can't get much easier or more efficient. At least not until they can wire directly into our brains.

If you want to *do* something, get up and go do it. You're not 5. The people in your life are not your mother or your maid.

If you have lazy people in your life, you can make your life and theirs better by weaning them off taking the easy way. It might hurt a little at the beginning, but it'll pass. It's like (yet another) old saying: Give someone a fish and they eat for a day, but teach them to fish and they eat for a lifetime.

When my kids were little, we did as little as possible for them. This isn't to say we didn't provide all the love, resources, and opportunities we could to give them the best chance in life. We did that part. But we wanted them to learn to be self-sufficient and independent humans. After all, they'd be leaving the nest someday, so it made sense that we focus on them being competent.

So they had to fill out their own forms, and we would sign. They had to learn to feed themselves, answer their own questions, and generally deal with stuff. And it worked. They are highly competent humans. The only downside though, is in their re-telling of the story, we raised them as feral children who had to fend for themselves. If either writes a book, I don't think Mom and Dad will come across as wonderfully as we think we should. Ah well. So it goes.

In your life, whether the lazy one is you or people around you, there's a cost to leaving things the way they are, a cost to enabling them or being enabled by them. It stifles growth, and it hampers development of life skills that save a lot of headache and misery down the road.

If it's them, work to stop holding their hands. Answer their questions with your own, such as, "I don't know, what do you think it might be?" or one of my (admittedly sort of snarky) favorites, "I don't know, what did Google say when you asked?"

If it's you: Be a grown-up; don't be a child. It's not a good look. Do it yourself. Do your homework, then go ask questions if you need more. Go look it up.

Chapter 63: Signal in the Noise

Suppose your boss tries to chew a new hole in your body about sales or some other metric he sleeps with at night being down 1% in June. And you think, "Yeah, dum-dum, it happens every June when people start taking vacations and worry less about our product. It's normal."

That's "noise" in your data, not "signal," to borrow an idea from people who watch radar scopes. "Signal" refers to a meaningful change in the data, whereas "noise" is usually what looks like signal but is really variation that's just random or for reasons that aren't relevant. Examples such as this are a big reason why we factor in seasonality and other expected impacts to our data. It keeps our data normal, and it helps keep our bosses (or us if we're the bosses) from losing their minds and making everyone start jumping through unneeded drop-everything sorts of hoops.

Even when you don't explicitly factor in expected impacts, we often do it in our heads automatically, like ignoring that one-point drop in June. It's normal variation in the data.

The June sales example isn't random (which makes it less like "noise" but I include it here because like noise, it's the sort of change in our data that we ignore or accommodate, not react to).

Sometimes the variation doesn't have a known cause, but it does happen regularly, so we still can discount it as an expected variation in the cycle.

Now don't get me wrong, sometimes variation, whether predictably cyclical or not, is still bad. You just might not know yet *why* the variation occurs. It doesn't mean that it's not important.

What we're getting at here are the types of variation that don't really matter, whether they are random or whether they are explainable movement that you can't control (like the seasons).

In data analytics and in process-improvement work, we look for the normal range of some activity, then we try to teach people to focus on the ones that are *outside* of the normal range.

Sometimes, tiny variation *is* bad. We have essentially a zero tolerance for plane crashes in the U.S. When you look at Six Sigma process improvement, you typically look for no more than 3 defects in a million in a traditional production environment. That varies a lot depending on how refined the process and the product are – and the cost of mistakes – but very few industries really expect to get to zero. But we don't like it at all when passenger planes crash. Even though if we had a few a year, it would still be an insanely small percentage no matter how you measured it: flights, passengers, miles, whatever.

The point still holds, though. It's just that the higher the cost of failure, the higher the cost of being wrong, the tighter you draw limiting boundaries on the variation you'll accept.

That point sends us to another, and it's the biggest takeaway for this chapter: Make sure the effort you are putting into whatever number you are chasing – sales, defects, clicks, engagement, whatever it is – is worth the cost you put into it. That can be staff hours, money, frustration, burnout, turnover, all sorts of costs.

There's a classic called the Pareto Principle. More informally known as the 80/20 rule. In simplest terms, it's that 80% of the problems will be caused by 20% of your customers. Or 80% of your management time will be sucked up by 20% of your staff. Or 20% of your staff will do 80% of the work. Or 20% of your customers will generate 80% of your revenue. You can see how this applies in almost as many places as you can think of. And no, mansplainers, it's not a rigid ratio. It could be a bit more or less. It's an idea.

This 80/20 perspective can be huge. Sometimes letting that one employee go who is just the worst brightens the world tremendously for everyone else. Sometimes it brings clarity to who you want to focus on as customers.

Learning to set the boundaries of what you care about – and learning the discipline to ignore the variation outside of those boundaries – will help you stop wasting time and money chasing metrics.

This applies outside the office too. You know that 80/20 holds in relationships, friends, and family. I know you do. Neediest friends. Most difficult family members.

And learning about signal in the noise is a bit like some ideas you've already heard, like don't sweat the small stuff, or worry about only what's in your control, or don't chase perfection. These are all variations of good advice that allow you to focus on what's worth your time – and be a little more chill about what's not.

Chapter 64: Argue the Other Side

Our country is so politically divided that for too many of us, once you know where someone gets their information, you already think you know whether you can talk to them; you already know what they probably think on just about anything.

How do we even talk to each other? The best advice I've seen is that we can't convince each other with facts and reason (which hurts my nerd soul). We have to do it by building connections, by building relationships. We listen more to those closest to us, to those in our groups. Beating each other down with data doesn't work.

After we worked on avoiding the trap of binary thinking in Chapter 59, Nonbinary World, I want to drive down one particular lane of usefulness: To be able to Argue the Other Side.

Here's what you do: Pick any issue that matters to you, and argue the opposing view to a friend who will suffer you while you go on about it. Take abortion for example. This is a tough one for a lot of people, not only because many are either absolutely convinced of one position or the other, but also because there are lots of people who are sort of one position or the other, but are generally uncomfortable about it. Like it's an issue without an ideal answer.

But let's say you believe firmly that women have a fundamental right to make choices about reproduction. Make the case why it should be restricted or controlled. And if you believe deeply that it should be restricted or controlled, make the case why it shouldn't. Whichever view you have, if you can't articulate an opposing viewpoint, why can't you? Do you refuse to try? Do you honestly not understand why someone might feel differently than you for reasons other than ones that would be insults?

It's easy to write off people as ignorant, sexist, racist, misinformed, whatever it may be that fits the "villain" in your story. It's easy – and it's often true – but that's almost beside the point here.

What we believe is right and true, and what we believe to be the terrible failure of the other side, are both bolstered by all sorts of biases. We know what we know, and how smart and amazing we are. But from our view, everyone else is dumb and misinformed, and easily swayed.

What can we gain from doing the work to argue the other side, to be able to do it? It teaches us perspective.

It teaches us there might be a point in someone else's position, even if you are just convinced they are totally wrong.

The skill will help you grow as a human. It can help your outlook evolve, become more nuanced and useful.

For me, I read news sources that I don't agree with. I talk with people all the time with outlooks different from mine. I listen. Since politics, culture, and societal issues are part of my nerd wheelhouse, I do this sort of thing a lot.

Find the ways that work for you. It can be strange, like an expedition to unknown parts. Pack a lunch and dive in. Get your field glasses and a notebook, and figure out how to Argue the Other Side.

Chapter 65: It's a Measure, Not a Target

Measurements are useful, but when they become your target – your goal – they often are no longer useful metrics. On top of this, we naturally optimize the activities we measure, so if we look at the wrong things, we will often go about our day the wrong way.

How is this relevant here? Make sure your target – your goal – is the right one. Then let the metrics you use guide and inform you on the way to that goal. An everyday example: You might want to be healthier, not to lose weight. If being healthier is your goal, then your weight, the foods you eat, how much you eat, and your activity, can be your metrics. But if losing weight is your goal, there are ways to do it that are unhealthy and won't last. This idea holds true pretty much everywhere in life.

Another example we hear about a lot: standardized testing in our schools. For all the value in knowing how our kids, the teachers, and the system are doing, if we end up in a place where there's a tendency to teach to the test itself, almost no one wins from that. Teachers are hamstrung, the kids aren't learning what they should, and we all lose.

And if you peel off a few more layers of the onion, you often find that we measure things that we *can*, and we don't capture other metrics that we *should* because they are tough to measure. We end up placing more value on what we can measure, and we devalue "soft," hard-to-capture data. Even the name "soft skills" (social and interpersonal ones) for example, can have a dismissive or negative feel when those are the skills that allow so much of everything else to actually work.

In student testing, it became common to measure teacher performance based on test scores. Why? Because we have the data. We've learned over time that this is a bad idea for a whole range of reasons, especially that each teacher isn't given the same type or set of students as all the other teachers. So those test scores miss all the variation influenced by things like parental education and income. But when a different approach was advocated, say, having teachers observed and graded while they were teaching, then issues of reviewer bias come into play (I like this teacher and not that one). And like the "soft skills" mentioned earlier, think about how time-consuming and expensive it would be to evaluate that way. So, yep, we measure what we *can* and ignore what we can't.

It means we need to find ways to measure health, not just weight; or the health of families, not just their income; or the gains our students make, not just their test scores.

It means it's on us to make sure we are separating the goal we have from the metrics we are using to track progress. And it means it's on us to make sure we are finding a way to measure what we really need, not just what's easy.

Chapter 66: The Pool

Chapter 54, Out Front, started by noting how most companies and organizations responded during the pandemic and the racial unrest that rocked the U.S. in 2020. When the realization dawned that two of the most important things to me in my coaching and analytics work – leadership and data – are key to finding solutions to disparities in our society, I knew this book would be the right place to talk about both.

Here in this chapter, we focus on the relevance of one important aspect of data. Why data? I often think about these issues in terms of "The Pool," the availability of something or someone that's important to an issue.

We already know some things. Women and people of color are underrepresented in many areas of society. They are underrepresented as CEOs and in corporate boardrooms, in the judiciary and in legislatures, as professors and engineers – the list goes on. If you want to make a difference, to start working together on what to *do* about these issues, I argue that it's helpful to look at the data to see where the biggest source of an imbalance starts.

For example, anything we look at involving women and men should be split about 50/50, because that's how we split in the population. Same with Black Americans, but at about 13%. So any time the ratio is different, *something* is going on. Not automatically bad, malicious or intentional, but *something*. Our nation's judiciary is just one example. About half the judges should be women. But data shows at the state and federal level, women hold about a third of judicial positions. That's a big enough difference that's unlikely to be random.

So where does The Pool come in? Start looking upstream in any process. Where are judges drawn from, and how are women represented there? How's the balance in law schools – and in the universities that feed the best law schools?

Look at prison populations as another example. At the federal level, about 38% of inmates are Black Americans, far outpacing the 13% you would expect if they reflected our society. Where did this "pool" of criminals come from? How did they get to that point? In this example, you could start looking at differences in policing, in the judicial system, in the educational opportunities, in family resources, and in institutional and societal structures.

Once you let the data show you where the problems start to build, it can guide you to the areas with the largest potential for change. In the case of prison populations, the answer to address the imbalance might not be to let criminals go free, but to target where the imbalance starts in the first place and focus our resources there to address it.

This holds for all sorts of social issues we face, including corporate leadership, wage inequities, health outcomes, and the list goes on. One of my favorite coaching questions is "What problem are you trying to solve?" When it comes to society, these questions can be big, complex, and often seemingly too hard to do anything about.

So look at the data, and let it guide you to *where* you can be most effective in bringing about change. This is a great way to help get started on working to make things better.

Chapter 67: Attack the Message

Why are so many people, often men, so angry all the time? They act like such a-holes.

I don't know why I'm not numb to it yet, but often I will dip into the comments on a social media post, and it stuns me that people are just mean. They insult the writer as spectacularly as they can. Seems like almost a sport to see how deep you can cut someone, how clever you can be, not in your counterargument, but in your insult.

Even setting aside all the people who are just mean – those who attack the messenger – we see those who seem to revel in cutting down an argument. But not in a way that is constructive to refining the original idea, but more so to demonstrate how much smarter, more clever, more knowledgeable the attacker is than the "ignorant fool" who posted the original thought.

Then you add on top a brutal attack on anything that's seen as different. What you look like, who you love, how you express your faith, or any number of things. And if you're a woman or person of color, you get all the "bonus" attacks about who you are, what you look like, and what these men think should be done to you.

We can explain a lot of this away by acknowledging a loosening of norms about what you can and can't say in public. What seems coarse and unnecessary to one might be real and honest to another. But that's only some of it.

It's pretty widely understood that people can act all big and tough from a keyboard, when it's not in person, especially when the user feels anonymous. Then stir in the sexism and racism that was already there, and it would be easy to wring our hands and give up.

What you *can* do is lead by example. First, of course, don't do any of this yourself. Even if you are an awesome human, sometimes we slip or get goaded or super angry about something we are passionate about. So vigilance is required.

Second, stay away from the worst places that foster this. The more of us who do that, the more the world of awful humans becomes isolated – a world unto themselves in a way. A world full of people away from us, ostracized as they should be. And by avoiding outlets, places, and organizations that actively foster or allow hateful things, we let the marketplace of ideas, the capitalist notion of competition, drive winners and losers. And in that optimistic future (we have plenty of dystopian futures written for us), the hateful people are minimized and sidelined as much as possible. Made irrelevant, hopefully they wither on the vine.

Third, and this one is harder, we have to actively oppose all that is angry, mean, and hateful. Standing up. Speaking out. Those are scary, and risky. The scary part you can get over. For the risky part? You have to figure out your own tolerance and preserve your own safety. But we still have to stand up, so look for ways to reduce risk by banding together to stand up to bullies. We learn to fight them on our terms, not theirs.

Once you make attacking the argument your default, your norm, then we can get more comfortable actually doing it. Give yourself permission to disagree – and to voice a contrary opinion. Give yourself permission to question the arguments and ideas of others.

At the same time, we learn to give space to everyone else (except the bullies) to allow arguments, to allow contrary and opposing views, without jumping to conclusions that the speaker/writer is racist or sexist or ignorant or somehow wrongly biased by their perspective.

We allow ourselves this grace in our own opinions and beliefs, yet many of us are reluctant to assume anything but the worst about others. Let them demonstrate by their words and actions who they are. Let them be innocent until proven guilty. What we ask for ourselves, we should afford to others.

Don't crucify or jump to conclusions. Let people make their case, then ask questions to see where they're coming from and what they mean. And if they prove their ignorance, their bias, their malice, still attack what they say, not who they are. It takes a lot to be better. But it's worth it.

Chapter 68: Zero-Sum Game

In the world of data and analysis, "zero-sum" means one person's loss is another's gain. Whatever the outcome, the positive and negative add up to zero. Another common variation is the "win/lose" situation. It is the default outlook, the default strategy, for a lot of people. They have to lose for you to win.

Think about all the examples we hear about winning. You crush your enemies. Bury them. Destroy them. Humiliate them. Make them cry. We use terms of war, and phrasings that are just plain mean. We *love* to win. It's built into our American DNA.

There's nothing wrong with winning, with having a strong drive to succeed, to best the others, to be on top in your field and in your endeavors. I think it helps us as a nation and as a society to push boundaries, reach new heights, find new answers, and to grow.

You can win, you can just *kill it,* but that doesn't mean you have to gloat or be a giant jerk about it. My modest proposal is to do it with class, to do it with grace. When you show some class in your victory, you show something better about yourself to the world. When you choose words to define your efforts and your contest in terms that a Decent Human Being would use rather than the language of a brute or a bully, of someone with no taste or class, you make everything around you better.

So look for the "win/win" strategy. Pay them for a patent that you want. Reward them for the idea, and then go profit from it. That's win/win. Or, maybe you find a way to steal it legally and give them nothing. Well, aren't you a big shot? Yeah, that's win/lose, and you don't have any real friends, just those who hang around for your scraps pretending to like you.

If you can't find a win/win strategy, seek restraint and kindness with your victories. When you take a ship in battle, don't throw the crew over the side; put them in lifeboats with some food and water. Imagine how those on the losing end might feel if you actively work to minimize the cost or the pain to them.

And when it goes the other way, be a grown-up in your losses. Don't blame everyone but yourself. Don't pitch a fit. Nobody likes a tantrum or whining from a 5-year-old. We like it even less coming from an adult. It is not a good look.

You know what's a good look? Graciousness. Like when an athlete praises the performance of the losing team – and sounds like she means it. Like when an athlete shares the credit for victory with others and doesn't instead explain why it was all him.

In some ways, this is all about being a good sport and not a sore loser. But I am pushing to expand the idea of this to everyday life – as a way to level up.

Chapter 69: A World of Difference

We talked throughout the book about differences and why they matter.

Even though each trait or group might be small in number, they add up. It's not one human who is gay, neurodiverse, nonbinary gendered, brown, non-Christian, with parents from another country.

No, it's not White, Black, other. It's not hetero or gay. It's an entire range of things beyond White, European-centric, mainline Christian. It's a whole bunch of humans who are all a little different in a rainbow of ways.

You might be able to talk yourself into thinking any one of these groups is so small that you can ignore it, that its members are outliers, so we don't need to think about them or change anything we've been doing.

I don't think the size of a group matters, because in the end, we're all still human. But if you do, then I am arguing that there are so many small groups out there, that as a real and practical matter, we end up with a society made up of differences, not one big group and everyone else.

You can go to lots of places in the U.S. and see all White faces. So the idea of being a non-White-majority country can seem weird or fake or far off. But if you look at data, and I love data, you see lower White birthrates and lots of non-White immigration. You can draw a line and see where it goes. The 17 and younger part of our population is already majority non-White. Today. Right now.

Traditionally, "difference" was suppressed, and people who stood out were punished unless they were powerful enough to be left alone.

Every immigrant group, every non-Christian, or even non-traditional-Christians: They all have their stories of being "different" in America, stories that often revolve around just how hard society made it for them.

Catholics and Jews experienced it; waves of Chinese, Irish, and Italian immigrants did, too. Then those from Central and South America. All different, all with stories of how they paid for being different.

As we see more and more diversity in faith, skin color, culture, professions, values, gender, sexuality, and as many other ways as you can think of, the challenges and the stories ring familiar as the ones from generations past.

And we always seemed to struggle with it, to handle it poorly. In the 1960s when men started growing their hair long, they were ridiculed, sometimes beaten up, for it. Seems silly now. But change the time, and the thing that is different, and it's the same story over and over.

Much of this is who we are as humans; it's how we are wired. We want stability and predictability. It's how we've built our lives and how we've survived. The Sun comes up; the weather is generally what we expect. The seasons come as planned. The Moon cycles every month. We don't like change. We just don't.

This means – assuming we don't evolve a new outlook anytime soon – that we need to look inward to adjust and expand our idea of "normal," and not keep looking outward expecting others to conform. That's the big takeaway here.

Think about this world of differences as something to celebrate. It's a mindset shift, but really, it's an easy one if you can get your head around it. These differences are not something to tolerate or endure; they are something to adjust to, and learn to accept as normal, not strange, and fundamentally, to see as valuable.

Think about how much easier your life will be if you aren't stressing about different people and different things. Think about how much better *their* lives will be if they are not being bullied or ostracized.

Think about all we get from this diversity. Hell, even diversity has a bad undertone for too many people. It's become a weapon in a political war. It's one of the reasons I went with the idea of "differences." I don't want to be part of that war; I want to be part of the celebration. Join me.

Chapter 70: Giving Back

When was the last time you did something for someone else (someone who doesn't live with you)?

When was the last time you did something for someone else and didn't expect anything in return?

Why should you give back? Because helping others is the right thing to do. The thing that Decent Human Beings just know and don't need more of a reason. And it's also because others have probably helped you in small ways or large. Giving back is a way to repay that, to contribute back to the society we live in.

After I wrote that, I stared out the window for a while, thinking through all the ways the world has helped me so far. It's easy to think you've done it all on your own, that nobody helped you. But sometimes the ways are subtle, small, almost unnoticed.

My list is long. The first summer job I had, the one that meant so much to the person I would become, was a funded program to help kids. I had student loans that helped me get through college.

I had a world of amazing people and groups show up to help when my wife was in the hospital. I was scared and had two toddlers whose needs didn't change because my life did. A friend from work showed up with a giant platter of peanut butter sandwiches. She didn't want Dad and the two girls to starve. We ate them all. I never forgot that act of kindness.

Another army of help showed up later when one of my girls got hit with leukemia. Family, friends, strangers, people driven by faith, by caring, by love. It brings a tear to my eye just sitting here writing this.

There's so much more, but I just wanted to start. Now I ask you to do the same. Stop for a few minutes and think of the ways the world has helped you, large and small. This is *why* we give back.

What does "giving back" mean to you? I think it varies a lot depending on where you are in life, and the value you place on service, a value that often comes from how we grew up and the experiences we had. It also varies depending on what sort of human you are. The more empathy you have, the more you will care to help others. The more you are connected to those who need help, or have been there yourself, the more you will want to do something.

For some, giving back just meant they could check a box on college applications. Maybe later it was some small chunk of time or money given to seem like you care or to fit in at work. For some people this means they are so focused on their own life that they just don't think much about others. For some people, they really don't care all that much about anyone other than themselves and those who can help them achieve their goals.

This is a spectrum, a bell curve, like so many other things we've talked about. So I want to talk to you on the extremes, and the rest of you in the middle.

On one end of the bell curve, there's that wonderful human who never says no. She is forever helping someone. She gives her time, energy, and talent nonstop. She is amazing, and she is exhausted, and she always puts her own needs last. She's been doing it this way for so long, I don't even know if she can imagine putting herself first, much less doing it without feeling selfish.

Everyone in the world around her is special and is well taken care of. But for her? No one does anything or even thinks about it. She puts herself last, and so does everyone else. It all seems normal. But it's not.

If you are this person, work on putting yourself first a little, just a little, here and there. Work on saying no. Get some sleep. You can't take care of anyone if you collapse and die, right? So take care of *You.*

If you know this person, do something for her. Ask her how you can support her. Say no the next time she offers to do something that helps you. Do it your damn self.

On the other end of the bell curve is the selfish one. He thinks only of himself, and that only a fool would do any different. The world is hard, and you have to fight for yourself and take what you need. Helping others is a waste of time. If people really need help, it's for the government, churches, or nonprofits to deal with.

If he gives at all, it's money, not time, and it's to look good or score points or to get ahead. If he does give his time, it's for the marketing value of the effort. And it better be worth it, because he is busy and important. Time is money. Relationships are transactional.

If you feel this way, I hope it changed some as you read this book. I hope you see an opportunity to be a better human. You'll feel good, so you still get something out of it. Help someone. Help a group that does something you care about. That will make a connection easier and make you more likely to think the time spent is worth it. Do something for the sake of doing it, not the credit for it you want on social media. Just try it.

If you know this person, work to nudge him in a better direction. Make it easy for him to take the steps. Lead by example, but try to do it in ways he can relate to. Running off to the Peace Corps will be alien to him – a thing other people do. But if you get him to donate some time helping with financial literacy at a community center or whatever his Master of the Universe skillset is, he'll be more likely to see himself there.

If you're in the middle, sort of muddling along, doing what you can, when you can, that's great. I appreciate you. For you, my advice is to think about what's important to you in the world and what skills you have, so you can target your efforts more effectively. It will help others more, and if you are more efficient, you can do more with less of your time and money. It will still fit in your busy life or within the limits of your purse.

And for all of us, think about being more intentional. There is a seemingly never-ending need out in the world, and it can feel overwhelming, even pointless, to even bother. Try to look at it this way: Everything you do helps someone. If you helped someone be safe; be supported; be more healthy; eat a meal; have a bed; get help with a physical, emotional, or mental need, that is enough. Don't get lost in the world of so much unmet need that's still there. Think about the people, even one person, you helped. It's enough. It's a lot. If we all helped one person or did one thing, imagine what the collective impact would be.

You can help foster arts in the community. You can help make the Earth healthier. You can give back through your own expertise and professions. Be a mentor. Be a Big Brother or a Big Sister. My point is that there's a way that will work for you. This is another one of those things that isn't one-size-fits-all.

No matter where you are in your journey, the time is now. You might be able to give more of your time when you are young or when you are older, you might be able to give more of your wallet when you are in the middle somewhere, but don't let that stop you in the now. You can always do something, even something small, to help one person, to do one thing. It's enough, I promise. Just do it; just give back.

The Wrap

I hope you got something from this book of Human Training, even a single "a-ha" moment. If something in here made your life better, we both won.

It took me a year start to finish to get this book ready, and it means the world to me to share the work I do in a way that's accessible to everyone. I am grateful that you are reading it. Thank you.

I wanted to do a Top 10 list that summarizes the entire book. For two reasons: to give you something to share to that friend who won't read anything longer, and because the challenge would be fun for me, and it would force a focus on what I am truly getting at. OK, that's 3 reasons, I know, I know.

It wasn't easy getting 70 chapters down to a Top 10 list. I got to 11, close enough. Here's a crack at it:

1. Put your phone down and pay attention to the person you are with, or the thing you are doing
2. Do your damn job. The world is counting on you. You get paid for it. It's really not that much to expect
3. Do what you say, and own it when it doesn't work or when you screw up
4. Take the back seat sometimes, let others shine, and learn that it's not always about you
5. Try hard things and scary things. Be curious. Evolve. Don't get stuck. This is how we grow
6. Take the time to recharge, the time to live well
7. Learn to read the room and when to shut up and listen. Learn what empathy can do for you – and for everyone else
8. Don't try to fix everything. That's not what we need from you all the time. Encourage, enable, support, and mentor others in fixing things themselves, and along their journeys in general

9. Don't be an ass or a dark cloud, and don't hurt people
10. Learn about the world. Don't be stupid. Care about something (besides yourself)
11. Your perspective is not universal. Remind yourself of this all the time – and constantly strive to manage your biases.

One of the most important things for me, layered under most of life, is to be able to laugh. Things are funny. Laughter is healthy. (Just not at the expense of others, right? We learned that, right?) And most of all, be able to laugh at yourself and along with others laughing at you.

As a bonus, it is powerful and disarming when you agree with the jackass taking a shot at you. "Your family doesn't like you!" he says. "I know, right!" you exclaim with a smile, "Nobody does." Where's he gonna go from there? You won and he looks like the petty little thing that he is.

Anyway… Back to the point. The entire point. Be a Decent Human Being. This book is a guide to helping you be better, and to make it easier to manage all the drama, all the hassle, all the frustration and all the joy, that comes from everyone else.

Also, call your mother.

About the Author

Chuck McDanal lives in Florida with his wife, Cynthia, a clinical psychologist. They met when he worked in Washington, D.C., after graduate school and thought she was a brilliant city woman. The brilliant part was true, but it turns out she was a rural Central Florida native who fishes better than most of the good old boys. He is still holding a grudge over that bait-and-switch.

They have two daughters, who both graduated from an International Baccalaureate program. One is a graduate of UC Berkeley who is now in a Ph.D. program at Stony Brook, and one is studying at university in Germany.

Chuck is an avid runner who has completed 11 marathons, including qualifying and running in the 2019 Boston Marathon. He also ran the New York, Chicago, and Marine Corps marathons, as well as a 50k (31 mile) trail race. He is a huge coffee fan who has been roasting his own beans for the past 10 years in roasters he built himself, but now has a commercial roaster to take advantage of the profile data it provides.

Chuck single-handedly renovated his office building as the latest in a long string of exciting personal challenges that included rebuilding old motorcycles, sports cars, and a giant military vehicle. He collects antique safes, has a tool for just about anything, and names everything.

He travels the world, loves old cities and their museums; has dived reefs off the coast of South America, skied back-bowls all over the West (and in the Swiss Alps), jumped out of airplanes, and off a mountain in Alaska. As a kid, he grew up in California and New Hampshire. As a teenager, he dropped out of school and wandered the country, working on a fishing boat off Cape Cod and living in a remote shack on the Pacific coast in Big Sur.

In his community, he has served on the local newspaper's editorial board and the board of the electric utility, as well as the boards of multiple nonprofit organizations, and the Chamber of Commerce. He has also served on the boards of the Lakeland Symphony Orchestra; Lkld Live, where he is past president and board chair; and the Lakeland Runners Club, where he is past president.

He is a graduate of Leadership Lakeland Class XXXI and Leadership Polk Class X, and he was Chair-Elect for Leadership Lakeland Class XXXVI and Chair for Class XXXVII. He is a member of the Lakeland Rotary Club, and has served as a board member and chair of the Communications Committee. He was honored as 2020 Businessman of the Year by the Lakeland Chamber of Commerce.

The shortest version of the professional stuff: Chuck is the owner and manager of Studio C Solutions, an organizational optimization, data analytics, and coaching firm. He also is the vice-president of Kindelan McDanal & Associates, a psychological counseling and testing practice.

Additionally, he owns StudioChuck, a commercial property holding company, and Chuck Roast, a boutique coffee roasting business. Previously, Chuck was president and general manager of LkldTV, an internet-based TV station. He joined LkldTV from the Ledger Media Group, where he was the Director of IT & Operations, and earlier was a group operations director with The New York Times Co. He also worked as an editor in The Ledger's Newsroom. Prior to moving to Florida, he worked in Washington as a researcher for the U.S. Sentencing Commission.

Chuck holds bachelor's and master's degrees from Virginia Tech, is a Certified Analytics Professional, has a certificate in Business Analytics from the Wharton School of Business, served in the U.S. Marine Corps, is a Six Sigma Black Belt, and an RRCA-certified running coach.

www.ingramcontent.com/pod-product-compliance
Lightning Source LLC
Chambersburg PA
CBHW022046020426
42335CB00012B/576
* 9 7 9 8 9 8 5 3 1 4 5 0 2 *